OF BURMA'S FAMILY TREE

D1485699

PRINCE ALBERT OF SAXE-COBURG AND GOTHA 1819-1861

Princess Helena
1846-1923
m
Prince Christian of
Schleswig-Holstein
1831-1917
(5 children)

Princess Louise
1849-1939
m
John, 9th Duke of Argyll
1845-1915

Prince Arthur
Duke of Connaught
1850-1942
m
Princess Louise Margaret
of Prussia
1860-1917
(3 children)

Prince Leopold
Duke of Albany
1853-1884
m
Princess Helen of Waldeck
1861-1922
(2 children)

Princess Beatrice
1857-1944
m
Prince Henry
of Battenberg
1858-1896

Grand Duke
Ernest Louis
of Hesse
1868-1937
m
Princess Eleonore
of Lich
1871-1937

Princess Alice of Hesse
1872-1918
m
Tsar Nicholas II of Russia
1868-1918
(5 children)

2 others

Alexander
1st Marquess of
Carisbrooke
1886-1960
m
Lady Irene
Denison
1890-1956

Princess Victoria
Eugenie (Ena)
of Battenberg
1887-1969
m
King Alfonso III
of Spain
1886-1941

Lord Leopold
Mountbatten
1889-1922

Prince
Maurice of
Battenberg
1891-1914

George,
2nd Marquess
of Milford Haven
1892-1938
m
Countess Nada
de Torby
1896-1963

LOUIS, EARL
MOUNTBATTEN
OF BURMA
1900-1979
m
EDWINA
ASHLEY
1901-1960

Grand Duke
George Donatus
1906-1937
m
Princess Cecile
of Greece
1911-1937
(3 children)

Prince Louis
1908-1968
m
Margaret
Geddes
1913-

Lady Iris
Mountbatten
1920-
m
Michael
Bryan
(1 child)

Don Jame
Duke of
Segovia
1908-
m
Countess
Emmanuele
de Dampierre
(2 children)

Don Juan
Count of
Barcelona
1913-
m
Infanta Maria
of Spain
1910-

3 others

Prince Philip
Duke of Edinburgh
1921-
m
Princess Elizabeth
1926-
(1952 Queen
Elizabeth II)

Lady Tatiana
Mountbatten
1917-

David, 3rd Marquess
of Milford Haven
1919-1970
m
Janet Bryce
1932-

Lady Patricia
Mountbatten
Countess
Mountbatten
of Burma
1924-
m
Lord Brabourne
1924-

Lady Pamela
Mountbatten
1929-
m
David Hicks
1924-

Don Juan Carlos
King of Spain
1938-
m
Princess Sophie
of Greece
1938-
(3 children)

3 others

Lady
Joanna
Knatchbull
1955-
m
Baron Hubert
de Breuil
1956-

Lady
Amanda
Knatchbull
1957-

Hon.
Philip
Knatchbull
1961-

Hon.
Nicholas
Knatchbull
1964-1979

Hon.
Timothy
Knatchbull
1964-

Edwina Hicks
1961-
m
Jeremy
Brudenell
1960-

Ashley Hicks
1963-

India Hicks
1967-

MY MOUNTBATTEN YEARS

MY MOUNTBATTEN YEARS

In the Service of Lord Louis

William Evans

HEADLINE

First published in 1989
by HEADLINE BOOK PUBLISHING PLC

British Library Cataloguing in Publication Data
Evans, William
  My Mountbatten years.
  1. Great Britain. Mountbatten, Louis
  Mountbatten, Earl, 1900–1979
  I. Title
  941.082′092′4

ISBN 0–7472–0142–0

Typeset in 12/12½ pt English Times by
Colset Private Limited, Singapore

Printed and bound in Great Britain by
Richard Clay Ltd, Bungay, Suffolk

HEADLINE BOOK PUBLISHING PLC
Headline House
79 Great Titchfield Street
London W1P 7FN

To the memory of
Lord Louis, Nicholas,
Lady Doreen, Paul Maxwell
and Twigga.

Also remembering so many wonderful friends who were
the victims of such violence in Northern Ireland,
especially Billy and Nessie Mullen
at the Enniskillen Cenotaph in 1987.

Contents

Acknowledgements viii

List of Illustrations ix

Prologue 1

Chapter One: Jam Jars from the Cemetery 3

Chapter Two: Corned Dogs, Pussers Kye, Salmon
and Strawberries 15

Chapter Three: Full Fig 31

Chapter Four: Ban-yans and Fans 43

Chapter Five: Wellington Boots and Iced Lollies 67

Chapter Six: On the Move Again 95

Chapter Seven: Gold Teeth, Beatles Wigs and the
Revolution That Never Was 115

Chapter Eight: The Big Man of Queenie 133

Chapter Nine: A Blue Lobster 149

Chapter Ten: Mullaghmore Revisited 163

Epilogue 167

Appendix One: Beds I Have Slept In 168

Appendix Two: A Selection of Lord Mountbatten's
Uniforms 172

Appendix Three: Lord Mountbatten's Robes 175

Appendix Four: A Complete List of Lord Mountbatten's
Orders and Decorations 177

Index 179

Acknowledgements

The author would like to thank the following for their help with the book:

My dearest godson Andrew James Auty, who so persistently inspired me to write this.

David Benedictus and Karen Ross of Kingston Books 'who put me together'

Lord Brabourne and the Broadlands Trustees for their kindness.

Dr C. M. Woolgar, archivist at Southampton University Library, for his kind and patient help.

Joseph and Pamela Harris, for listening and helping me with 'the big words'.

Peter Pugh-Cook, for the dreaded profile photo on the front cover.

A special big thank-you to Headline, in particular to Sue Fletcher and Sally Holloway who so expertly guided me to authorship.

List of Illustrations

(*Between pages 54 and 55*)
The evacuees at Helperthorpe Vicarage (author's private collection)
The author at eight (author's private collection)
Helperthorpe Vicarage (author's private collection)
Hall-boy at Knapton Hall (author's private collection)
My first bicycle (author's private collection)
The petty officers of the Royal Yacht *Britannia*, 1960 (author's private collection)
My first world tour with Mountbatten, New Zealand, 1961 (author's private collection)
Lord Louis and Solly Zuckermann at the Borneo war front, 1963 (Imperial War Museum)
En route to Nehru's funeral (reproduced by kind permission of the Broadlands Trustees)
Lord Mountbatten, New Guinea, 1965 (Broadlands Trustees)
Author, Australia, 1965 (author's private collection)
Author, Otehei Bay, New Zealand, 1965 (author's private collection)
Author, Tahiti, 1965 (author's private collection)
The presidential palace, Monrovia, 1964 (author's private collection)

(*Between pages 118 and 119*)
Lord Mountbatten at a Mexican rodeo (Broadlands Trustees)
Lord Mountbatten on the steps of the Ministry of Defence, 1965 (Broadlands Trustees)
Lord Mountbatten presenting standards in Germany (Broadlands Trustees)

LIST OF ILLUSTRATIONS

The sword table (Broadlands Trustees)

The Green Room, Broadlands (Broadlands Trustees)

Broadlands (Broadlands Trustees)

The cinema, Broadlands (Lord Brabourne)

The Duke and Duchess of Windsor arrive at Southampton (*Southern Evening Echo*)

Classiebawn Castle (author's private collection)

Lord Louis on *Shadow V* (author's private collection)

Shadow V, Mullaghmore harbour (author's private collection)

Lord Mountbatten and the Hon. Joanna Knatchbull (Broadlands Trustees)

Shadow V (Broadlands Trustees)

The Duke of Westminster's yacht, *Trasna of Ely* (author's private collection)

Prologue

August Bank Holiday, Monday, 27 August 1979, was one of those idyllic days with cloudless skies, warm and balmy. I was on the terrace patio of my home on a small private island nestling amongst a cluster of islands on a lough just near the Sligo/Donegal border. The world seemed at peace and I was at peace with the world as, deep in my own thoughts, I settled down to some weeding. Cookie heard the terrible news on the radio and banged on the window. I rushed indoors and she told me what the BBC had said.

A few miles away was the Bay of Donegal, which has some of the most exciting coastline scenery to be found anywhere in the world. Out in this bay, a fine-looking and dignified man of seventy-nine had been enjoying the last day of a short summer holiday, pottering around in a boat called *Shadow V* with his lovely family, and hoping that the lobster pots they had laid down earlier would supply them with a lobster or two for tea. The Atlantic, which could be very violent on that stretch of coast, was glassy calm, the Donegal mountains and the clear blue sky reflected in its waters.

Without warning, an almighty explosion ripped apart the sweet old boat which had carried the family so faithfully over the years. The old man was floating dead in the water; his grandson, a charming and lively boy of fourteen, dead; a twin grandson, blown clear, was injured and dog-paddling for survival; a fifteen-year-old boy on his school holidays from Enniskillen for a summer pocket-money job, dead; the daughter and son-in-law floundering, severely injured, but alive; a dear old lady over eighty, the daughter's mother-in-law, would die a short while later after a vain struggle to hold on to life; the

1

tiny dachshund dog, the daughter's pet, dead too in the sea.

Within seconds the boat had been shattered into fragments; all that remained was debris, mutilated bodies, spreading ripples – and confusion.

So ended the life of one of the nation's greatest human beings: Admiral of the Fleet Earl Mountbatten of Burma, Knight of the Garter, last Viceroy of India, former Chief of the United Kingdom Defence Staff, Colonel of the Life Guards, Colonel Commandant of the Royal Marines, Governor of the Isle of Wight, Chairman of the Council of the United World Colleges, active member of well over two hundred organisations including the All-England Lawn Tennis Club at Wimbledon, the Magic Circle, the Society of Genealogists, the British Burma Society, founder of the Royal Naval Film Corporation, proud holder of the Order of Merit, former Supreme Allied Commander South-east Asia and honoured by virtually every country in the world, a man who had devoted his entire life to humanity, a life senselessly and tragically cut short by mindless terrorists. This was the man whom it had been my great privilege to serve for ten years of my life.

That evening, after I had wandered round my small demesne in a stunned daze, slowly trying to come to terms with the saddest day of my life, I stopped at a favourite spot which looks down on the broad lough and its scattered islands. There was a fantastic sunset as I gazed in the direction of Classiebawn Castle, so near, but blocked from my view by a mountain. A shaft of light rose directly towards the heavens, and in the remarkable silence unique to that part of Ireland, I felt the spirits and souls of Lord Louis Mountbatten, Nicholas and Paul ascending into Paradise. I stayed where I was in floods of tears until it was quite dark. I had wanted to be with them to see them on their way.

Chapter One:
Jam Jars from the Cemetery

My grandfather came from the Rhondda Valley in South Wales, but moved north to Durham to work in the vast steel mills where he became, and my father after him, a 'top-puddler' or steel shingler. Puddlers wore special waistcoats to denote their rank, and their skilled craft of forming the steel was handed down from father to son. I was born in Durham during the great industrial depression in the North of England of the 1930s. I was three years old when my family moved south to Hull, in Yorkshire, where my father took up work with his former manager, who had asked him to join his mills there.

Wages were not high in those hard times and we were a large family of ten, of which I was the youngest and the seventh son. We were often pretty hungry and poor but, thanks to the dear Sally Anns (the Salvation Army), we did at least have a hot meal every Thursday when my elder brothers would take me by the hand (I was only four or five years old) to the hall to be fed. Perhaps this is why I have always felt a particular respect for the Salvation Army ever since.

My mother's background could scarcely have been more different. Her family were Gibraltar hoteliers who ran one of the colony's principal hotels. It was when my father was Provost Sergeant just after the First World War in the garrison there that he met her and wooed her.

I don't remember my mother too well. In the first week of the Second World War, I was sent away on evacuation and both she and my father became ARP wardens. (Father was too old for military service, but he had fought in the first war.) During a bombing raid my mother was directing children into a shelter, and there was one child who obstinately refused to go in. While she was ushering the child to safety, the blast from a nearby bomb hurled her against a brick wall. She lived on for a few years but was, as they say, 'bomb-blasted'. My father died many years later of pneumonia, following an industrial accident at the steel mills, at the age of seventy-six.

I was a proper little city tyke, an Artful Dodger. When I was about five years old, I was appointed police look-out for the older kids when we went to the Saturday afternoon matinees at the local cinema. Being a very poor family, my brothers and I had no ready cash for the cinema, so we had to find ways of raising some. The older boys used to scour the city cemeteries, looking for jam jars on the graves. These jam jars – only the sound ones, they were useless if they were cracked – were our cinema entrance money. They were valued at a penny a jar. Things were made very much easier for us when the iron railings around the cemeteries were removed: though we did not realise it at the time, they were, of course, being melted down to provide tanks and ammunition for the war. I hope we were forgiven by the Almighty for nicking the jars from the graves!

It cost us one jam jar to get inside the cinema; the other would buy us a long roll of liquorice with a hole running through it and a small bottle of fizzy pop. We would unroll the liquorice and drop it into the bottle, then nibble and suck – sheer bliss! What a little terror I was!

On the outbreak of the war with Germany, I was six years old. It was a bleak September morning in Hull, and they lined us up in the yard of my infants school. What was it all about? An outing? If so, why were so many mums and dads gathered there to see us off – not mine, however – and why were so many of them in tears? I stood there in utter confusion.

At the school gates were rows of Hull City double-decker buses, and the reassuringly familiar figure of the school caretaker. But there were tears in his eyes too, and that was *not* reassuring. Next to him were some enormous wicker hampers.

These he opened and withdrew small canvas sling bags which he placed over our heads. On each bag was a label identifying our school. Already we bore proudly attached to our clothes large luggage labels with our names on – not that many of us could read them. And then there were all those suitcases. Did we need suitcases for a picnic? Yet, if it were not to be a picnic, why did they give us bags of food? Mine included sandwiches, a bar of chocolate and a banana. I especially remember the banana, because I sat on it and it melted into the chocolate in the train.

At the City Paragon railway station the buses pulled up alongside the impressive steam trains, waiting to take us on the next leg of our mystery trip. A mystery trip indeed; few of us had even seen a train, let alone travelled on one. With a wheezing, a hissing and a puffing, we rolled out of the city and into the beautiful countryside of South Yorkshire. We were all thrilled.

As the light began to fade from the sky and we were still travelling, some of the children realised that they would not be home for supper. They started crying for their mothers, and I believe that I did too.

My two elder brothers and I were being taken away from home and we didn't know where and we didn't know why. We were frightened and nobody had told us anything. We were too young to understand anyway.

After many hours, we came to the station at Malton, a small market town in the heart of the Yorkshire wolds. We disembarked and were shepherded along the platform to where people with lists endlessly checked our labels and put ticks against our names. At Malton was a smaller convoy of single-decker buses, and it was here that I was separated from many of my schoolfriends. Most serious was the parting from my two elder brothers, who, being members of the senior school, had been taken to another part of Yorkshire. My three eldest brothers were serving in the Army: one with Monty in the desert of North Africa, one with the paratroopers, and the other was a Green Beret commando.

My destination was the small farming community of West Lutton, whose village school hall was the 'evacuation and distribution centre'. In charge of the arrangements was the local vicar of Helperthorpe, the Revd E. L. Dawe. Small groups of farmers and their wives arrived to take charge of their allotted evacuees – two or three to a family. The vicar called out the names, the farmers responded, the children were led away, until I was left alone in the hall, lonely and unclaimed.

For what seemed like a lifetime I was carted up and down garden paths in the middle of the night and watched the Revd Dawe knock on front doors. But everyone in the district had already taken more than they had agreed to. There was nothing for it but for me to spend the night at the Helperthorpe Vicarage with the other two evacuees, also from Hull, already in residence there. In the morning things could be sorted out once and for all. They never were and I stayed.

The evacuations were expected to be temporary. It would only be a few months before Hitler and co. got their come-uppance – everybody knew that. I doubt whether anyone – and certainly not my well-intentioned evacuation officer – would have believed that the war would last six years. Or that the large and rambling vicarage would be my home for the next eleven and a half years.

My guardian, the Revd Leslie Dawe, was a charming man, fair, loyal but of the old school and very formal. Poor Hull children were cheeky tykes, and we were no exceptions, but, though he ruled us with iron discipline, he never once raised a hand to us. A Cambridge man, an MA, he had never married, and was looked after by a housekeeper, Mrs Pearson, a widow, with her son Stanley. If the Reverend was our surrogate father, she was our substitute mother. We were brought up very strictly, but with great care and kindness, though without the love of a real family.

The vicar's mother and father, whom we called Grandma and Grandpa, completed the household. Grandma was a right old dowager, very regal. Grandpa was a retired vicar. They were well into their eighties when I arrived and sadly neither lived to see the end of the war. I remember my old pair of corduroy shorts and how Grandma used to patch them with pieces of pink satin nightdress. The next day at school, the schoolmaster would twitter and giggle – and at the time I had no idea why – perhaps it was the huge white frock button which dear Grandma had sown on to my fly front!

I shared a room with my fellow evacuees, the brothers Mulvaner, and I expect we tested the vicar's patience to the full. But, thanks to Leslie Dawes's firm handling, it was not long before I became a perfect little gent.

We were sent to the local school at Weaverthorpe, the next village, where you might have mistaken us for refugees, for we had brought nothing with us except what would fit into a small suitcase. In mine was a pair of cotton shorts and a shirt, the sum total of my worldly goods. We walked up the valley to school each morning and back each afternoon, collecting the milk from the farm. Even when we got home, we still had the chore of bringing in sticks and coals for the fire. Only too vividly I remember how the snow would pack up the legs of my shorts, for the winters were severe in those bleak Yorkshire wolds.

One of my other jobs was to go round the local houses collecting ration books so that my guardian could buy extra corn for the chickens. (How I hated cleaning out the smelly chicken huts every week-end and dusting them with DDT!). In return for their corn ration, the people received eggs from us. Rationing was quite severe – clothes as well as food – and the petrol ration would only stretch to one shopping trip a month. We would either go to Malton, some fourteen miles away, or Scarborough, two miles further.

We evacuee children formed a tiny clique in the corner of the playground, until eventually we became accepted into village life. We learned to speak broad rural Yorkshire. We picked potatoes with the local lads and at harvest time helped with the threshing machines. Riding home on the huge Dale horses at dusk, I would try to emulate the old farm hands and ride a sort of sidesaddle – these magnificent animals were so broad-backed, it was almost impossible to sit astride them. Sadly, as we neared home, the old horses would start to trot and I was slowly but surely bounced right off, mercifully missing the pounding hooves. Now I had to run behind them the rest of the way home, as they would not stop until they had reached the farm.

All the chickens at the vicarage had names. One of them

was named after a schoolmistress who had been brought out of retirement to teach us. That was the chicken which one day happened to get a piece of bread stuck down her throat, and I went rushing indoors to get my guardian: 'Hurry, hurry, Miss Smith is choking in the drive.' And out he came flying, fully expecting to see the poor old schoolteacher.

I was very happy at that little local school and did well there, especially in drawing, maths and English. At the tender age of eleven I also managed to play the church organ for services.

Occasionally there were bombing raids near us. Even though we were a hundred miles from Hull there were aerial dog-fights and one night a cluster of bombs fell in our kitchen garden. Fortunately it was a huge kitchen garden and the whole pattern of the bombs fell away from the vicarage and down the fields. I well remember the day a couple of Messerschmitts flew over the village – there were army manoeuvres in the area – and ripped up the main street with machine-guns. Naturally we boys rushed out of the house to see what was going on, but our guardian grabbed us by the scruff of the neck and hurled us back indoors. We were most upset to be missing the fun.

In the evenings we listened to Churchill on the old crystal set as he crucified that 'horrible little guttersnipe Hitler'. We shall never forget the inspiration we got from this.

Stanley, the housekeeper's son, who was eighteen, was in the Home Guard. He was a lovely lad, but so slow, so slow. He soon got us three evacuees polishing his brass, polishing his boots, polishing his gun, polishing everything, including his tin hat. There we would be down on our knees trying to get him togged up for the parade, buckling up his stiff canvas leggings, fixing his cross webbing, and my guardian would watch and say: 'Oh come on, Mr Hitler will have been and gone before we get Stanley ready!'

At last Stanley was ready and off he would tramp on his merry way down to the unit, with his tin mug and his billycan clanking away at the back of him, his gun slung over his shoulder, a sight to scare the daylights out of any Jerry paratrooper.

Air-raid wardens were sent up into the belfry of the nearby

church where the bells hung silently, waiting to ring them in the event of an invasion. Sometimes we children would take turns up there, hoping against hope that Jerry would come, so that at last we could ring those beautiful bells. But we never heard them until the Armistice was declared.

I only went to see my family for one week-end during this time, about six months after I left Hull, but the bombing that night was so severe that we were immediately returned to the country. Hull suffered more than its fair share, because of its steel mills, its dockyards and its position on the North Sea coast. One of my brothers cycled over to see me once or twice, and my guardian made me write home regularly, though I never received any replies. The war had made communications difficult, of course. There were no letter boxes then, and very strict rationing of petrol. All road signs were removed in case German paratroopers landed.

Whatever the reasons, I gradually lost touch with my family. When the war was over and I returned to Hull to attend the local secondary school for my final academic year, our old house had gone and my family, although I lived with them, were virtual strangers to me. In fact, we lost three homes during the war and each time my guardian would break the news to me, jokingly adding that clearly Mr Hitler had our name in his book! But it would be misleading to suppose that I was homesick. I loved the country from the start and hated the city, especially now that it was in ruins from the saturation bombing.

I must have been about eleven or twelve when the vicarage, being the largest house in the neighbourhood, was commandeered by the Army preparing for D-Day and the invasion of Europe. The General, no less, moved in with his ADCs and what seemed like hundreds of soldiers. This was excellent news. Now we could go to school by tank, by bren-gun carrier, or even – thrillingly – on an army motorbike. In return for the use of the bath, we were given tins of steak and the children in particular were spoilt with chocolate from the American GIs. We also had a standing invitation to the mobile cinema, where I watched, entranced, the adventures of my favourite film stars, Charlie Chaplin, Douglas Fairbanks Jnr, Roy Rogers with Trigger and the Lone Ranger with Tonto. Little did I think . . . but I musn't get ahead of myself.

Even in that small village school we were made to sing the National Anthem every morning in assembly; I doubt whether the majority of schoolchildren today even know the words. Of course the Anthem was played on all public occasions then, at garden fêtes, at the cinema, and every night when the wireless finished transmitting its programmes. I'm eternally grateful that I was brought up to respect my King and Country and had instilled in me at an early age the great national pride which seems so lacking in today's world.

At the age of fourteen, my formal schooling and the evacuation scheme over, I returned to the vicarage. Now a job had to be found for me, which would provide a roof over my head. I had always longed to make a career in the Merchant Navy, but in those days no one could afford the money it would cost to send me to Pangbourne for a training cadetship.

My guardian arranged for me to be taken on as hall-boy at Knapton Hall, a large country house nine miles away, across the wolds. The house belonged to the Grotrian family, who owned and ran a number of Scottish newspapers. The mistress was a very prim and proper Scottish lady, something of a tartar, who reminded me of the late Queen Mary.

I had been brought up to be very self-sufficient and to take my full share of helping in the home, from making my own bed and laying the meal tables to cleaning fires and the other many household tasks, so it came very easily to me to accept going into service, which was, in the late forties and early fifties, still regarded as a major source of work. What is more, I had no false pride whatsoever about serving others: my guardian had brought me up to have total compassion for everybody and everything, so never for one moment did I consider anyone to be other than a fellow human being whom I had no shame at all to be working for. As children, we would serve table (after a fashion) to the adults, so I found the whole idea of service completely normal. When, later in my career, I came to serve great world figures who by the nature of their jobs did not have time to take care of their homes or lives or day-to-day tasks, I took enormous pride in my calling.

At Knapton Hall, I was given a bedroom at the back of the house and outside my window was a sloping roof to the ground. We were forbidden to be out after 9.30 p.m. Consequently, the young maids used to come through my bedroom and use this unconventional exit when they wanted to get to freedom and the late-night dances in Rillington, the largest village in the area. I would put their bicycles in the spinney outside the garden gate before I locked it, and they would return at about two in the morning and climb back in through my bedroom window. The housekeeper never found out.

I was paid fifteen shillings a week all found, a good going rate, and I worked directly to Mr Tassell, the butler. (Whenever he was asked whether there were two Ls in Tassell, he would reply: 'Yes, there are, but I shall only go to one of them!') Besides Mr Tassell, there was a housekeeper, a cook, four maids, a chauffeur, a gardener and me. Not a grand establishment, just a normal Yorkshire country house.

We were like one big happy family, although discipline was strict. I remember distinctly one hot summer's day when I had removed my tie for the long cycle ride with the post and, quite inexplicably, the mistress appeared down the back drive. 'Go and put your tie on, Billy,' she admonished me, 'and don't let me catch you again without it.'

I rose at five thirty a.m. to collect the wheelbarrow and spade, for my first duty was to clear the hearth of the huge tree log which would have been burning on its gimbel chain for the past twenty-four hours. Then the hearth would have to be cleaned and polished with Cardinal Red. At six, I would fetch in the kindling, the coal and the logs, stoke the boilers, and then go down on my knees to scrub the stone-flagged front hall. By eight, I had to be clear of the downstairs. My next duty was to lay out the butler's morning clothes, complete with clean starched collar and tie. A substantial cooked breakfast was waiting for us at eight thirty, by which time I was certainly ready for it!

After breakfast I would assist in the pantry, fetching and carrying and carting the heavy trays up and down the stairs between the dining-room and the kitchen. For the first year at Knapton Hall I was not allowed on any pretext to touch the silver without chamois gloves. Then I would clean and polish the butler's 'cuddy', the room where he and the housekeeper sat and ate. Staff lunch was at midday. After the dining-room lunch, I cycled three miles to Rillington with the mail, bringing back any shopping. The butler's tea had to be prepared, his evening tails laid out ready for when he changed for dinner at six p.m. Dinner meant more tray-carrying up to the big dining-room and down the stairs again. My official bedtime was nine thirty, with a ten o'clock deadline, but by then I could hardly keep my eyes open.

Mr Tassell, the butler, was more thorough than any lord would have been and it was from him I received the basic training that would stand me in good stead for the rest of my life. I treated him as I would a lord. I never saw the ladies' and gentlemen's dressing-rooms until after my first year's training and I never entered the dining-room whilst the family was eating. I neither smoked nor drinked, and was allowed out only on Wednesday afternoons. My favourite recreation was boating on the lake behind the gardens.

It was while I was at Knapton Hall that I fell in love for the first and only time.

Her name was Brenda and she was the daughter of one of the dailies. I was fourteen and she looked like a very young version of Grace Kelly. She had two gorgeous blonde pigtails and she was the sweetest girl I have ever come across. She said to me once: 'You never argue with me,' but, as far as I could see, there was no way she could have done or said anything wrong. I was besotted.

It was not easy for us to meet. I used to sneak out when I could and meet her at the churchyard on the estate or sometimes in the church, which I had to keep clean and tidy, the only place where we could be safely alone. We were very polite about it, of course, but when we were together we held hands. Sometimes I would play the church organ to her. That was our courtship, and how we spent most of our precious moments together. It was the loveliest and purest of all love affairs. I never even thought of any other girl and have not seriously done so since. Sadly, we were never to marry, but I have loved her all these years, all of my life. The permissive sixties were not yet with us, for which I am eternally grateful. Courtship in my day was such a sweet and innocent friendship, and you really got to know and understand each other, a feature so absent today, which is why, I think, we see so many divorces, separations and unhappy marriages.

Chapter Two:
Corned Dog, Pussers Kye, Salmon and Strawberries

After three and a half years at Knapton Hall, I had reached conscription age at seventeen and a half and was required to register for National Service. My family were army folk. With one exception, all my brothers had chosen the Army. But I had a favourite brother, Joseph, who had been in the Merchant Navy. He had been killed in the early stages of the war at just eighteen years of age. As I have said before, I had always had a secret longing to join the Navy, to see the world.

It so happened that my employer's son-in-law was a captain, Royal Navy, and through him it was arranged for me to join the Supply and Secretariat branch of the Royal Navy as a steward, thereby putting to good use the training I had received at the meticulous hands of Mr Tassell.

When I left the house to go into the Navy it was without saying goodbye to those I loved, or was fond of. I've never been any good at saying goodbye, and become far too emotional – even to this day.

My initial six-week basic training was at HMS *St Vincent*, at Gosport. This was a period of being hauled out of bed at six in the morning, shouted at, given three minutes to complete a cold-water shave, shouted at, handed a lump of bread for breakfast, and shouted at again endlessly on the parade ground.

I recall being a part of a Royal Guard of Honour when a

very young Princess Margaret came to Portsmouth. Our best uniforms only arrived on the morning of the parade. As we were lining up on the parade ground the tailors were following us around pulling out the tackings and pins while we desperately tried to remember the sequence of orders to Royal Salute, present arms – up, two, three! – with our unfamiliar guns. The discipline was very hard and, although I was glad of it later, at the time I was ready happily to strangle my training chief petty officer.

It was while I was at the Royal Naval barracks that I found myself on a charge for the only time in my naval career. It was January and we were sleeping in Nissen huts – lying in bed, I could look up and see icicles forming. I was rash enough to cover my bed with my naval greatcoat as I couldn't sleep for the cold. When the patrol came round in the middle of the night, I was raked out of bed and put on a charge of incorrect bedding. Although I was let off with a severe reprimand, I had had to endure the unpleasant rigmarole of being on disciplinary charge; it was the only time I ever had to 'doff my cap'. The discipline was almost inhuman, but it worked! I was certainly glad to have been put through it later when I became a petty officer and had to impose such rules myself.

When the initial training was over, I was sent to Wetherby – back to Yorkshire of all places – to complete steward's training for HMS *Ceres*. It was not for long, though, and within three months of joining the Navy I was appointed to my first sea-going ship, HMS *Cadiz*, a battle-class destroyer in the 5th D Flotilla Squadron, to serve on the personal staff of the captain, Captain Bush, an old chum of Captain Cartwright, my former employer's son-in-law.

It was January 1950 when we left Portsmouth on a flat calm Sunday bound for Gibraltar. We were to rendezvous at Portland with the Home Fleet on a NATO joint exercise. This was just after the formation of NATO and it was the first time I had been to sea, other than a short trip on a pleasure boat at Scarborough. I thought it was Paradise.

At seven a.m. on the Tuesday morning as we sailed out of Portland Harbour with the NATO Fleet we received a warning of severe weather. By the time we reached the Bay of Biscay we were in the middle of the worst gale in Biscay for seventy years. For five days the entire crew just longed for death. I had to report on our condition to the Captain on the bridge (*Cadiz* had an open bridge). All he said was: 'I can't understand what's wrong with the blasted ship's company.'

The seas were mountainous and from the bridge of a small destroyer it was like driving up a mountain in a car. Up and up on this moving mountainous mass, until suddenly there was nothing beneath us, and down we fell. Now it was downhill fast but we were sailing straight into another mountain. This one was right on top of us before we knew it, and we went straight through it. The waves washed over the *Cadiz*, its propellers out of the water, until at last they took a grip and we felt the shuddering which meant that she was on propeller power once more. Above and below deck, everything was wringing wet. Pure fear gripped us.

It was not just a matter of longing for death – we were convinced that we were going to die – but throughout all this we were having to perform the NATO exercises, playing silly sailors with the fleet. The only relief for me came when I tumbled into my hammock. The joy of a hammock in a rough sea is magical. You still get the yawing and the pitching, but you don't get the yaw, the pitch and the roll all at once. It is your only respite. However, no sooner was I in my blessed hammock than we would be blasted out by klaxon at two a.m. to action stations, the seas more violent than ever.

My action station was in the Forward A Turret Magazine, which is at the very front of the ship and right down below, the worst possible place to be when a ship is pitching. It must have been forty-five feet from the crest of the wave to the valley beneath, and we heaved and rolled and plunged and vibrated ceaselessly. It was necessary for us to be strapped to the bulkheads to avoid being hurled across the magazine. We could no longer tell whether we were the right way up, or upside down or what. Nor did we care. So miserable and lousy were we that we simply wanted to end it all.

Meanwhile, as captain of the A Magazine, my job was to operate the huge shell hoist which took the enormous 4.5-inch shells up to the gun turret above us. Each shell was locked by flip nuts into its individual 'pigeon-hole' and was both heavily greased and ice-cold because the whole system was refrigerated. And so were we.

Sick, sweating, covered with grease, frozen and tired, we had to lift these huge shells, almost three feet high, into the hoist. All around us was the vile stench of red lead paint and explosives while the ship reared and bucked like a mad steer at a rodeo. And God help us if we missed the hoist; God help us if we so much as dropped an eyelash into the magazine (a courtmartial would have followed); and God help us if the ship should be in an accident, because we were locked in and would be instantly flooded and drowned. After two hours of this we were stood down from action stations. I crawled back into my hammock at four a.m. At five thirty, the bosun's pipe woke me for the start of another working day:

> Wakey, wakey, rise and shine,
> The morning's fine,
> You've had your time,
> Now I'll have mine,
> Lash up and stow.

It was during that crossing of the Bay of Biscay, my first real experience of the sea, that I left those gentle Yorkshire dales behind me and became a man. I learned how terrifying the sea can be; it should never be underestimated. But I learned, too, how to conquer fear, which is the main reason for sea-sickness. I was to experience far worse conditions later on, but suffered not at all.

Several of our small lifeboats were lost in that storm, smashed and ripped to pieces. Butterfly steel nuts riveted to a hatch were torn off as if they were no more substantial than putty. I remember the Captain saying: 'I can't understand what's the matter with all you people,' but the moment he came below to his cabin he turned pea-green like the rest of us and said that he was needed on the bridge.

By the time we reached the calm of Gibraltar harbour, we were exhausted. None of us had eaten much, because even if we had had an appetite for it, hot food could not have been produced in those conditions. In Nelson's day they had more sense. In the old wooden ships like the *Victory* they used to have a hotpot of stew hanging over an open fire. But all the *Cadiz* galley could provide us with was 'corned dog (beef) sandwiches' and 'herrings-in', the last kind of food for a sea-sick sailor. The only thing we could manage to keep down was ship's biscuit, very heavy and dry. But we were young, healthy fellows, and we soon picked up, especially after a cup of 'Pussers Ki', the strong cocoa which was dished out at night during the Middle Watch and at most other times, too, and which was so strong that a spoon could stand in it upright.

We lived very close, about twenty-two of us in a small mess, and we ate and slept and lived our lives together in there. Some of the boys on the night watches were in hammocks trying to catch up on lost sleep, just above your head, while you were having your lunch. There was little living space in destroyers in those days. People had to sling their hammocks in passageways, and the hammocks were 'lashed and stowed' up around the gun turrets. But we were a nice bunch, blood brothers: the odd boozer, and the usual problem of smelly feet and smelly socks, but we learned how to handle that sort of thing. The comradeship was the finest in the world, and the thing I was to yearn for later more than anything.

It was now that my private service stood me in good stead. I was used to working long hours. I was used to rigid discipline. I had never been one for nights out with the boys, and what I had never had I never missed. The only thing I missed was Brenda, and I missed her dreadfully.

When, after six weeks at sea, some of my mates got drunk and visited houses of ill repute, I could not understand why anyone in their senses should want to. I visited one once with a gang of mates, and that was quite enough! Naval life is very different now. There are not so many ships or foreign stations. Sailors marry younger, and they are flown home regularly to see their families. The whole pattern of the Navy has changed.

After those hectic days at sea, it was a considerable relief to put down anchor in the beautiful harbour of Gibraltar. In those days, Britain still had quite a large Navy, and we, together with our NATO allies, made an impressive display. I do not know how many ships there were, but more than two thousand seamen turned up at Fleet Canteen for the traditional evening tombola sessions which were such fun.

However, there was also considerable sadness for me at Gibraltar. For, just as we set sail for Livorno in northern Italy, I received a letter telling me that Brenda was to be married, to another man. We had been apart for two years, but had corresponded faithfully. I wanted to do away with myself. All my souvenirs – a lock of her hair, a little ring, a photograph – I flung over the side into the Med. While I was standing there late at night wondering whether to throw myself in after them, the duty petty officer found me and, mercifully, took me away from the stern where I had cast dear Brenda overboard.

I never got over her. I didn't see her again for some twenty years. Then she told me that I had taken it for granted that we would get married, though she said I never asked her. But what could I have offered her? At eighteen I was in no position to marry her on fifteen bob a week and away at sea for two or three years at a time. Also, it was considered almost indecent in the 1950s to ask for a girl's hand in marriage before you had reached twenty-one.

Anyway, docking at Livorno gave me the chance to visit Florence and Pisa. From there we sailed to Nice, Monte Carlo and Cannes. We were flat broke but, in the most expensive part of the South of France at the height of the season, we berthed alongside the huge yachts of millionaires. There were parties and dinners on board *Cadiz* for governors, ambassadors, mayors and such. Naturally, after one of these formal banquets, we would get to dine on the left-overs from the Captain's table and did ourselves very nicely. I did not much mind the extra work, though it offended my professional pride that I had to make do with standard naval issue in place of the fine china, silver and crystal I had been used to at Knapton Hall.

Being on the Captain's staff, I had few opportunities to go ashore, but one night of shore leave I do remember. About fifteen of us from the *Cadiz* had visited Cannes casino. They had allowed us into the foyer, but because we were all in uniform we were not permitted entry into the gaming rooms. In any case, we didn't have a penny piece between us. (We were paid fortnightly and this was 'blank weekend'; in any case, as a leading steward with a single hook I was on less than £4 a week, although, because I neither smoked nor drinked, I was registered as 'TT', which meant I received an extra three-pence a day in lieu of my pot of rum.) So there we were, sitting with very long faces, watching the millionaires parading in and out, and one chap came out in a beautiful camelhair coat – he looked like an Egyptian prince – and he just flung all these chips at us. Of course in our ignorance we had no idea what they were, and we assumed it was some Middle Eastern kind of insult. Until one of the lads picked a chip up and asked the waiter whether it might be worth a bob or two. A bob or two? It was a £25 chip, and that was a fortune to us on our meagre pay.

Then followed the biggest scuffle in the history of the Navy as we scrambled for multicoloured money chips around the floor of the casino. A very kind gentleman, the man in the camelhair coat, although we never had an opportunity to thank him, and never discovered his identity.

From the South of France, the *Cadiz* was sent to Malta, then in the throes of riots by Dom Mintoff's gangs, so we found ourselves in boots and gaiters guarding the dockyard and assisting the police to control the street riots. A more pleasant port of call was Cadiz, Spain, after which our ship was named and which she had not visited before. We were welcomed with a splendid round of civic balls, parties and dances. In return, we welcomed groups of schoolchildren, the disadvantaged, and the City Fathers, on to the ship. There were football and cricket matches and free transport around the city.

During my time on HMS *Cadiz* I must have been doing things right. My report claimed that I was polite, courteous and smart, but in truth it was natural to me. Again I was grateful to Mr Tassell for having done his stuff. And the consequence was that, after a brief spell in naval barracks, I was appointed to the retinue of Admiral Sir George Creasy. He was one of the loveliest of men, a grand old seadog with magnificent grey sideburns, one of the old school. He had just been appointed Commander-in-Chief, Home Fleet.

In normal circumstances the C-in-C, HF, would fly his flag on the flagship of the fleet, and the flagship in 1953 was the battleship HMS *Vanguard*. But circumstances were not normal, for King George VI was dying of cancer. *Britannia* was not yet in service, so the *Vanguard* was taken over as the Royal Yacht, and the King and Queen and the two young princesses sailed on her to South Africa in the hope that he would make a recovery in the sunshine.

Ironically, we were to benefit from these tragic events because the Admiral's quarters on board the *Vanguard* were transformed for the King's use. The ladders were removed and replaced with a most beautiful oak staircase. Enormous state rooms and cabins were constructed with glorious teak carvings. Everything that could be done to transform a battleship into a Royal Yacht was done, and, when the King later became too ill to travel at all, the *Vanguard*, improved and beautified, became ours once more.

She survived as the Royal Navy's last and greatest battleship, before they broke her up. I was so grateful to have a chance to sail on her. We travelled to the Arctic and beyond, through the mountainous seas that had given such a battering to the poor Russian convoys during the Second World War. In the course of our exercises in the Arctic we fired the fifteen-inch guns, the only time they were ever fired. Each shell weighed a ton and the whistles through the air were very weird and haunting, lasting what seemed like a full minute as they flew away into the gray wasteland.

While the King and Queen and the princesses were on board the *Vanguard*, we transferred to the temporary flagship of the Fleet, HMS *Indomitable*, one of those huge aircraft carriers, and quite a contrast to *Cadiz*. Everything on the *Indomitable* was on a much grander scale, with the added excitement of the planes landing and taking off. There was so much space that we were able to play three hockey matches simultaneously on the flight deck. One advantage of being on an aircraft carrier was that we received our mail more regularly than if we were on a smaller ship. From time to time, I was lucky enough to fly off with the Admiral on visits to other ships and establishments. There were more royal visitors, more dignitaries, more entertaining, more excitement. But the regime was, as ever, extremely strict. On a small ship, commands were relayed by bosun's pipe. On a carrier, they came by Tannoy and bugle, and we jumped to it.

I still only had the one hook – Leading Rate – and I worked with the retinue directly under the Admiral's secretary, who had the rank of Captain. There were eleven of us in the retinue, and our duties were to ensure that everything ran smoothly. We had to be there, but not be seen to be there. The moment the Admiral appeared on deck, everything would come to a standstill, even if he was in plain clothes to go ashore for a game of golf. Wherever we went, cannons boomed, guards of honour came to attention; it gave me a great thrill. We even had our own Royal Marine Band on board.

After the King's death, we had transferred the flag of the C-in-C, HF, back on board HMS *Vanguard* in time for the Coronation Fleet Review at Spithead in the Solent in the summer of 1953. Quite an experience! There were some 360 ships, battleships, aircraft carriers, destroyers, submarines and minesweepers, ships of all sizes from all the Commonwealth and foreign nations, and a whole column from the Merchant Navy, including the South Atlantic liners and seven of the big Cunarders. Lord Mountbatten had brought over HMS *Surprise* from the Mediterranean, where he was C-in-C, to be fitted out as a reviewing vessel because the Royal Yacht was still not ready. A glassy canopy had been built, and it was from this that the new young Queen and Prince Philip reviewed the fleet.

Our responsibility was alarming, because we were to coordinate the whole extravagant spectacle, a sight seen only once in a lifetime, and our place was at the head of the battle-line. Not only that, but we were playing host at a banquet for the royal party and the captains of all the ships. The wardroom was inadequate until we knocked down a few bulkheads, but the structural problems were insignificant compared with the logistics of serving this, the largest banquet held afloat this century. There has been nothing like it since, and I doubt we shall ever see such an assembly again.

We set up a system of traffic lights controlled by the Chief

Steward, with a code of flashing green, yellow and red lights to indicate when to move in, to lift, serve, clear and so on. We borrowed the best attendants we could muster from the Marines and from other ships. This gave us a complement of more than a hundred stewards and we trained them to help serve the banquet. We had to build special galleys with enhanced capacity and there were numerous rehearsals with a Wren officer standing in for the Queen and an admiral pretending to be Prince Philip. We even served them a substitute banquet. The evening before the real thing, a barge came alongside with tons and tons of roses, every colour known to horticulture, which had to be stored in the cold room overnight. A vast team of ladies was brought in just to arrange the flowers.

I've seen some sights in my time, but nothing to compare with the banquet and the review! There's never been a larger or more elaborate meal served on board any British naval vessel, and certainly never will be. The ceremonial silver and tableware was brought in from barracks, establishments and all over the fleet with a Nelson's Column silver centrepiece more than three feet high from Admiralty House. Everything we could 'pinch and borrow' was brought into service for this one occasion.

There were five courses – vast dishes of salmon, tons of strawberries – and the band played the traditional 'Roast Beef of Old England' as Her Majesty arrived at the banquet.

After the dinner, the highlights of the evening were the illuminations and the fireworks. The signal was a single rocket fired from the bridge of the *Vanguard*. Every ship had been wired, with the masts, guns, funnels, waterline, everything, outlined in electric lamps. After our rocket, every light on every ship was dowsed, and there was complete darkness for a minute. Then suddenly by a synchronised signal the whole fleet was illuminated. The hundreds of thousands of people up on top of Portsdown Hill had the best view, and they never forgot what they saw that night. Every ship, submarine, carrier, liner miraculously outlined – unbelievable! It was all too much for the BBC commentator who became so excited that he announced that the entire fleet had been 'eliminated'!

The shenanigans continued for weeks. The America Navy, the Canadian Navy, every conceivable foreign and Commonwealth navy was represented. On Coronation Day, the *Vanguard* sailed up the Thames estuary as far as her bulk would permit, and we sat on board and watched the Coronation on a television with a specially hired projection screen.

I would not have missed the Coronation for the world, but it gave us one hell of a six months!

In 1954, at the age of twenty-two, I was promoted to the rank of Petty Officer and went on an advanced petty officers' course to HMS *Royal Arthur* at Corsham in Wiltshire, where Prince Philip, then a lieutenant in the Royal Navy, had been an instructor. There were twenty-eight of us on the course and it was very intensive and very physical. We were split into small groups and given complicated practical tasks: how to get a three-ton lorry out of a ditch (we used blocks and tackle); how to rescue a trapped airman from a burning jet fighter; how to steal or recover a missing radar unit, represented by a keg full of wet sand over a branch of a tree seventy foot from the ground, that sort of thing. The culminating field exercise was that we would be taken in pairs in a closed truck to the middle of the Wiltshire countryside some fifteen miles from the camp and instructed to be back on base by six. But we had no idea of the direction in which we had been driven, and we were forbidden to touch any private property. We were allowed no money, no compasses, no watches, no aids whatsoever. All we had was our initiative.

The week prior to our course, another group of petty officers had been set the same task. Now they became our warders, hunting for us. The local kids were thoroughly educated in what we were up to. They were waiting in a reception committee by the Avon river, which we had to cross, and wished us a cheery good morning, commenting helpfully: 'That way, mister.' Since the pretence was that we were escaped prisoners-of-war, this spoiled the illusion rather and put us straight into the trap that our warders had set up. We were all captured.

At the end of the course (equivalent today to the SAS requirement), fitter than I had ever been in my young life, I rejoined the retinue of my old Commander-in-Chief, Sir George Creasy, now C-in-C Portsmouth and based at Admiralty House. Under Chief Petty Officer Zahra, a Maltese chief petty officer steward, Admiralty House was run with remarkable efficiency. At the age of seventy-two, Zahra was the longest serving CPO in the Navy. He was on his fifth five, that is to say his fifth extra five-year period after his regulation twenty-two years were up. He was very popular and celebrated for his expertise throughout the Navy and was the only man in the history of the Service to receive the long service medal twice. I learned a great deal from him.

At Portsmouth much of the official entertaining was done on board HMS *Victory*, Nelson's flagship, the most famous ship in Britain's glorious maritime history. I felt a very great sense of honour and tradition as I worked in the very quarters, in the great Day Cabin, that had belonged to Nelson. Honour and tradition is all very well, of course, but there were drawbacks. In Nelson's day, the average height of a sailor was about a foot below what it is today, and so the deckhead ceiling space on *Victory* was also about a foot less than it needed to be. Then there were these wretched big crossbeams in the Great State Cabin. One warned the guests, of course, but all they had to do was arrive and sit down and be fed while we, poor devils, had to nip in and out and round about, frequently carrying large dishes of hot food. Added to which, even though the *Victory* was in dry dock, there was the little matter of the eccentrically sloping decks. Next time you take a tour around the *Victory*, glance up and glance down and spare a thought for me . . .

In the next cabin was Nelson's hanging cot, a tiny little thing like a baby's cradle, which was actually where the great man slept. It may not have been haunted but we felt the spirits there. I was always excited and privileged to be working in such historical surroundings, in the very quarters in which Nelson had conducted the Battle of Trafalgar in 1805.

The Royal Navy is a very social institution, and enjoys its busy social life, its summer balls, its cocktail parties. There would be a dinner on board the *Victory* once or twice a week, and everyone who was anyone came. It might be a royal princess or a NATO chief or a Mexican dignitary, they all seemed to end up in Portsmouth. A very mixed bunch, but only the greatest VIPs got to dine on *Victory*. The others had to make do with Admiralty House!

Bulganin and Khrushchev came, the first time Russian leaders had visited Britain since the Revolution. And it had to be the only time in my naval career that I was taken ill with a throat infection. I was whipped into Haslar, the Royal Naval hospital, and the next thing I remember was being put into a glass cage – an isolation cage – with all these Russian admirals and doctors looking in at me.

In 1957, after completing my commission of two years with the C-in-C, I was appointed to the cruiser, HMS *Bermuda*. She was a beautiful ship, larger than a destroyer though not as large as *Vanguard*, and highly regarded by all who sailed on her. She had a cinema and her own band, which cheered us all up when carrying out tiresome tasks such as duty stations, transferring stores at sea, or taking on fuel from the Royal Fleet Auxiliary tankers. While she was being refitted in dry dock, I was drafted up to Hebburn Docks on Tyneside, where for three months I formed a part of the pre-commissioning crew, living like a docky in digs ashore. There was no comfort or luxury on Tyneside, but I counted myself enormously lucky to be amongst such kindly and genuine folk as the Geordies, and especially the dockies.

HMS *Bermuda* looked magnificent after her two-million-pound refit, and our first port of call was to be her home port, Bermuda, no less. Not only had I never been to Bermuda, I had never crossed the Atlantic. We had not been long at sea before we ran into a hurricane so violent that we had no choice but to heave-to and ride it out for four days. Otherwise there is no doubt that we would have foundered.

The damage to this glamorous vessel was horrific. The entire quarter-deck hatch at the stern, on top of the Captain's quarters and some forty foot above sea level, was stripped off in the middle of the night. We were taking in water at an alarming rate. Neither the fine teak panelling nor the cherry maroon carpeting took kindly to being washed in sea water, and the poor *Bermuda* looked like nothing better than a tramp steamer, rust everywhere and the fresh coats of paint stripped almost down to the bare steel. This would certainly not do for our home port reception, so all hands set to, including the skipper, and we repainted one whole side. Approaching Hamilton, Bermuda's capital, we looked fine, but if anyone had turned us round they would have seen what appeared to be a rusty sardine tin!

I suppose that second storm at sea, this time in mid-Atlantic, was more violent than the first, but the *Bermuda* was larger than the *Cadiz* so that, on the whole, life was not so uncomfortable for our eight hundred crew.

The island of Bermuda, though snooty, was beautiful, but when we reached the Leeward and Windward Islands I thought I had found Paradise. Of course, I was familiar with tropical islands from my cinema-going, but I cannot express adequately the joy I felt at actually being there, where the skies seem perpetually blue and the seas perpetually clear. Palm trees do something to me, bringing out in me the Robinson Crusoe character I often feel I'd like to be.

I was reluctant to come home, but strings were being pulled on my behalf and what was awaiting me in Britain was more glamorous and more exciting than anything I had yet experienced.

I knew that I was being put forward for the Royal Yacht by Sir George Creasy when I left his retinue. He gave me a fantastic personal write-up on my service records, and not many chaps had their service records written up in the personal hand of the Admiral of the Fleet and C-in-C.

On return to Portsmouth, we 'paid off' the *Bermuda* and I once more found myself back in the RN barracks in Pompey, wondering where my next draft would take me. I did not know for sure that I would get the Royal Yacht as, by that time, she had been commissioned. I was a petty officer now, too, which made it much more difficult since there are only twenty-six or so petty officers in the entire crew of two hundred on the *Britannia*. So, even though I had the personal recommendation of the only serving Admiral of the Fleet in the whole Royal Navy, I would need much extra good fortune to be with me. I need not have worried . . .

Chapter Three:
Full Fig

The message came through from my Divisional Officer that I was to report to him.

'Well,' he said, 'I see you're going to *Britannia*.'

He was delighted. But I was over the moon. I had arrived.

The Royal Yacht, *Britannia*, which had just recently been commissioned into service, was one of the finest and most up-to-date vessels in the world. It was the first new Royal Yacht since the *Victoria and Albert*. There could be no more prestigious appointment, and I could not believe my good fortune. All I had worked for was being rewarded, all my prayers had been answered.

I loved travel, but with the continuing reduction in the Navy's role in the world many of the wonderful stations such as the Far Eastern and South Atlantic were being withdrawn. The nuclear-powered submarines were being brought into service, and for them the Navy needed a new type of sailor, a technocrat and one who was prepared to live under water for six months at a time. But the *Britannia* was purpose-built to tour the world as a floating royal residence and gave great promise of wonderful adventures.

At once I embarked upon my required routine, the necessary barrack pit-stop clearances of medicals, X-rays, jabs and dental checks, as well as uniform fittings, which included the additional tropical uniforms that I should be needing. I was proudly sewing my special Royal Yacht badges on to my kit when I received an immediate summons to the Divisional Office one more.

With great trepidation I presented myself to the Lieutenant-Commander. He was so pleasant to me that my anxiety increased a hundredfold. What could I have done? Not saluted the quarter deck correctly?

'Sit down,' he said. 'Have a cup of tea. A fag?'

Good God, I thought, this is really serious.

'I've got some good news for you,' he said. 'You're going to Lord Mountbatten.'

I felt completely deflated. Shocked. Annoyed.

'No, sir,' I replied. 'I'm going to the Royal Yacht.'

'I'm afraid, Evans, his chap's gone ill, and you're needed as a temporary replacement for Lord Mountbatten's tour of Canada and America. You'll start immediately.'

I was furious. In my angry state I even told him that I wouldn't accept, although of course I was in no position to refuse. My heart had been set on *Britannia*, and now it seemed that I would lose my chance. It was well known that, once commissioned, the Royal Yacht would only make replacements 'on a dead man's shoes'. But my Divisional Officer promised me faithfully that, since it was only to be a short tour, I would be back by October 1959 in plenty of time to take up my commission on *Britannia*.

Partially reassured, I still felt extremely tense and anxious because everyone in the Navy trembled at the name and reputation of Louis Mountbatten – me included. He was the present First Sea Lord, the professional head of the Royal Navy, top dog.

This was to be the first and only pier-head jump (urgent posting) of my career.

So it was that, that same evening, I found myself whisked off with my full kit in a naval Land-rover to Broadlands, the beautiful house near Romsey that served as the country home of Lord and Lady Mountbatten. I was still smarting at my life being so disrupted just when I thought I had settled on the Royal Yacht. However, as soon as I arrived at Broadlands, I felt a nice warm glow of 'belonging'; I was immediately at home with my surroundings. Perhaps I was helped by my memories of Knapton Hall – although of course Broadlands is much grander and more magnificent. I consoled myself by thinking that at least it wasn't for ever and that this was certainly better than the barracks.

I was introduced to Lord and Lady Louis in the study. I instantly felt at ease with them. They were both utterly charming and unstinting in their apologies for upsetting my life as they explained about the sudden illness of the man I was to replace. (I later learnt that he had been afflicted by a severe case of Mountbattenitis, or stress.) They were of course well aware that I was due to join the Royal Yacht but they had selected me from my naval records. They could have picked any one of several petty officers, but I had clear advantages: I had been trained for the Royal Yacht, which meant that I was security-cleared and was considered suitable for royalty; I had previously been on the retinue of an Admiral of the Fleet and C-in-C, so had exactly the sort of experience they were looking for; most important of all, I was in barracks and available, then and there, to go anywhere and do anything.

I had seen Lord Mountbatten once before, when he had attended the Fleet Review dinner on board *Vanguard* with Her Majesty, but never for one moment did I think that I would now be joining his personal staff . . .

I liked him on sight; indeed, I liked them both. Of course, I was used to being in close proximity to VIPs, so I was unlikely to faint or freeze. Lord Louis, who had just been appointed Chief of the Defence Staff, told me that we were to fly to Canada (my first transatlantic flight) to join the NATO fleet on the newly opened Saint Lawrence Seaway. We would then take passage on board HMS *Scarborough* for an overnight sailing – not the easiest thing to organise when travelling with an Admiral of the Fleet *and* his Lady – to review the assembled fleet prior to his opening the huge Canadian National Exhibition. Prince Louis of Battenberg had opened a previous Canadian Exhibition, so it was fitting that his son should continue the family tradition. He was to produce for the organisers the same Gold Medal which had been presented to his father – a gesture which was to delighted the Canadians enormously. This was my first 'Don't Forget' item which I had to have ready at the appropriate moment – the first of hundreds.

I had so little time, and even less help, to get organised. The tour packing for Lord Louis was not even completed, and to take on such a task at such short notice was arduous in the

33

extreme. I had had no chance to get to know this man's personal habits, let alone the magnificent array of uniforms and the vast complexity of such matters as tropical whites, blues, ball dress, sashes, ceremonial swords and aiguillettes. We would need cine and still cameras, film stock and spare batteries, signed photographs and gifts for various dignitaries. And heaven help me if I forgot such little matters as the tiny folding spectacles, known as specklets, which were attached by a chain to his trouser pocket.

In short, I had complete responsibility for everything, both official and personal, required for this high-powered trip.

I think that what saved me was the speed at which everything had taken place, and the enormity and complexity of the task in front of me. I had no time to think, and no time to panic. Like everything undertaken by Mountbatten, the programme was timed with clockwork precision, and every minute was filled. This was principally a military tour, so the uniform requirements were paramount. Lord Louis wore American naval khaki, which I had not come across before, and a naval uniform which was far from the recognised model. But there would be numerous social functions as well as official ones. We would have to go straight into tropical clothes with white linen uniforms, suitable for Canada in August. But white is not the ideal colour when one is transferring in and out of destroyers and barges, and I soon learnt to always have a tin of blanco in my pocket to hide any black stains.

Lord Louis in his Full Ceremonial Whites was a magnificent sight, and worth all my trouble. He wore the blue sash of the Order of the Garter, the glittering diamonds and rubies of the Garter Star, the diamond star of the Victorian Order, and the glittering Star of India; round his neck he had the Victoria cameo diamond of the Star of India Grand Master's badge, which King George VI had insisted he should keep as the last Viceroy of India, and below this hung appropriately the American Legion of Honor neck badge. He wore the ceremonial Freedom of the City of London Sword, a naval sword embellished with his personal coat of arms in enamel, and the cypher of his South-east Asia command, a phoenix. I noticed a dent in the scabbard of this ceremonial sword and asked if I should get it repaired. At once I was blasted with an angry fusillade. Had I no sense of history? Did I not realise that that dent had been caused by an over-eager aide slamming the door shut before the Viceroy was completely in his carriage during the great historical farewell ceremony outside the Viceregal Palace in Delhi? It was therefore a 'historical' dent and not to be touched, though to me it was a serious blemish on his otherwise dazzling appearance.

When in full fig, Lord Mountbatten carried several extra pounds of precious metal about his person, which in hot climates would have sapped the energy of a lesser man.

Being so practical in everything, he devised many clever sophistications to his wardrobe to enable him to change quickly, an essential since he often had to do so eight times in one day.

For full-evening dress, the underpants were designed to be attached with buttons to the shirt tails. I would have one side already buttoned to form one leg. He would step into the pants at the same moment as thrusting his arms into the sleeves and hey presto! The shirt had its stiff high wing collar already sewn on with the bowtie in place and ready for tying. By the time he had fastened the bow I would have buttoned up all the remaining buttons down the front. Next came the socks which had garter-tops sewn into them and the calf area cut away so that they could not slip down his ankles. All his socks, made for him by Tenova in London, were designed in this way. Then came the trousers, with the braces sewn on and a zip fly. (Lord Mountbatten claimed to have been the first person to have zips sewn into his trousers.) As he stepped into them his arms would be out to receive the dress waistcoat on to which the sash of the required order had already been buttoned. These waistcoats were backless, so that, as he brushed his hair, I had the neck order in place and buckled him up the back. After this the high wellington patent boots, all ready with the pullers-on in place, and finally the magnificent braided tailcoat with aiguillettes, stars and miniature medals in place, speech cards in the breast pocket, a comb on a clip, also on clips and also in the breast pocket, Biros and fountain pens, on a chain in the trouser pocket the specklets together with a key, a ten-shilling note and five two-shilling pieces for tips for doormen and taxis in case something should go wrong with the car, along with two sucker tablets to ease his throat if he was to make a major speech.

The detail was extraordinary. All his shoes were handmade with small, counter-sunk rubber studs on the soles and heels which helped prevent slipping on wet marble or other treacherous types of flooring. When they were supplied with laces these would be made of elastic so that they did not require tying. (After the television series *The Life and Times of Lord Mountbatten* I received numerous requests for these laces from arthritis sufferers. They came from Peels, his bootmakers.) His neck decorations, the Order of Merit and the magnificent Diamond Cameo of the Star of India had gold clip-bars attached so they could slide quickly on to the shirt front, and not swing to and fro. (Our only problem with decorations came at the wedding of the King of Greece. Naval regulations rule that no more than four stars be worn at one time; with a special dispensation from the Queen, we were allowed to wear seven.)

His specklets (only required for reading) had side pieces which gripped the temples rather than folding over the ears, and had been designed to fold away neatly into a thumb-sized leather pouch attached to a chain and buttoned to the right inside pocket of all his trousers. The tiny key on this same chain was a master key which would open every possible lock that he might possibly need to open: despatch boxes, suitcases, front doors, gun cases, even the decorations case. Members of the retinue who needed keys had one which would only open those locks which they might need to open, and not any others. The whole system, devised by Chubb before the days of the microchip, was fiendishly clever, being both simple and secure.

We got things to such a fine art on that first tour of many that Lord Louis could do a complete change in ninety seconds flat.

This meticulous attention to detail was applied also to the office, where he planned a scheme to lick envelope flaps four at a time. Different types of letter required different-sized envelopes, of course, but it was vital that the secretary – or myself if I was sitting in for an absent secretary – folded the letters in the requisite way and with no more than the requisite number of folds. I soon learnt to cope with Lord Louis' exacting demands.

And so it was that, just two days after my summons to Broadlands, having spent one night afloat in HMS *Scarborough*, I found myself in the Royal Suite at the Royal York Hotel in Toronto, known to be the biggest hotel in the Commonwealth. There were five of us on the team and each of us had a suite to himself within the main suite. Truly this was the life!

Already, despite the meticulous planning, we were slightly behind schedule. It was hot and extremely humid. The Mayor, the Governor and assorted dignitaries were awaiting us in the anteroom; dear Lady Louis was in her slip, Lord Mountbatten was in his string vest. Suddenly he ordered us: 'Stop! Take your tunics off. Everybody take their tunics off.'

It was humid and tempers were fraying, so he ordered us to take a breather and drink an iced whisky. None of his immediate entourage was used to alcohol, and I hated it, so what with the panic and the effects of the whisky we soon became unsuitably hilarious. Increasingly it reminded me of a scene from Lord Louis' favourite radio comedy, *The Navy Lark*. Lady Louis, who had no maid with her, was trying to transfer her white St John's uniform buttons on to a clean tunic and Lord Louis kept sending me over to help her, while my principal concern was getting *him* into his white Tropical Day tunic, with which I was not yet familiar.

No sooner were they both togged up than I had to trot along after them with the next change which would be required for the National Exhibition opening and for which a full three minutes had been allocated. After a hectic four days and having spent three nights in three separate beds, I realised that this was going to be the pattern of things, but consoled myself with recollecting that it was only a very short temporary appointment and that in October I would be joining *Britannia* which would surely seem like a holiday after this! Not for long, not for long, was what I kept repeating to myself.

Lord Mountbatten, as I was beginning to realise, was a bit of a schoolboy at heart, and he could not conceal his excitement when he saw the gigantic rollercoaster at the exhibition.

He kept eyeing it and whispering, 'Oh, I'd love to get on that,' but of course in his Admiral of the Fleet uniform it was unthinkable. So, as soon as the formalities had been completed, we dashed back and changed into plain clothes and returned to the exhibition site, joining the back of the enormously long queue. Fortunately, his pictures had been splashed all over the newspapers and one of the officials at the fair recognised him, so we were taken through a side entrance. He had four straight goes on the rollercoaster, whooping it up like a kid, excited and happy. We all had to accompany him, but fortunately he insisted on sitting in the front car and we could hide ourselves away behind him. He was in his element; we were giddy and queasy. We were all very grateful to return to the tour programme, which did not allow for much more fun.

After two hectic days in Toronto, Montreal and Quebec, we headed off across America on a tour of the military bases, seeing the underground rocket sites and other top-secret establishments. We were accompanied by G-men, and the need at all times to be vigilant was something else I had quickly to accustom myself to.

Lord Mountbatten had with him a number of small despatch boxes containing top-secret defence papers which I was never on any account to let out of my sight. We had problems with the top American security man, who, having established that these despatch boxes contained top-secret information, would insist on piling three of them on top of one another in the middle of the room and sitting on them. Later, he handed them to Lord Louis (who was flabbergasted and looked at me as if to say, 'Who is this nutter?'), announcing obsequiously that they had never been out of his sight! I thought that our way of doing things was much to be preferred. No handcuffs, no fuss, I would just very quietly and very carefully take special care of the vital despatch boxes, as I would any particularly precious jewellery belonging to Lady Louis in a jewel case or in my pocket.

We were staying at the time in a really beautiful Spanish-style hacienda, a US military guest house within a heavily protected base. The place was so secure that when we arrived with this vast motorcade, complete with outriders, military police and G-men, not unlike a presidential procession, we were unable to gain admittance until the military policeman at the gate had saluted and we had all shown our passes. Nothing untoward about that, you might think, except that nobody had thought to mention the necessity of passes to any of us, and none of us had one. The American admiral accompanying the party had to vouch for us, and very amusing he found it too, but I can't say that the presence of at least fifteen security men made my job any easier.

Of course, the American security men had no idea how to cope with our protocol and were endlessly asking me what they should call the Mountbattens. Was it Your Majesty, Your Earlship, or Your Lordship? I was very tempted to tease them; they were so easy to impress. But I resisted the temptation and told them that in a military capacity 'Sir' would be quite adequate. Equally impressionable were the newspaper men. I remember in the Deep South being interviewed by a cluster of journalists about the suit Lord Louis was wearing. It was made of an experimental glassfibre material ICI had wanted him to try out, and questions were asked too about Lord Louis' tie. I explained the significance not only of that tie, which was his own CDS tie - maroon with a white shield of crossed swords for the Army, and anchor for the Royal Navy and an eagle for the Royal Air Force, surrounded by the garter *Honi soit qui mal y pense* and surmounted by the Elizabeth Crown - but of numerous others we had on tour with us. There were in the wardrobe almost four hundred of them, for which I had invented a system to make sure I knew which tie was what. This involved tags and a chart, and it was usually front-page news wherever we went. Some such system was essential, because Lord Louis would usually have to change ties about eight times a day, as he made it a rule always to be wearing the appropriate one. Such a small thing gave pleasure out of all proportion. We received numerous letters of appreciation, especially from the Canadian ex-servicemen who had spotted him wearing the correct regimental tie. The public rarely miss anything connected with royalty and can be very critical, so we were always extremely careful not to offend.

Intrigued as the journalists were with Lord Louis' wardrobe, it was mine which most interested them. I was wearing a striped shirt with a stiff white collar, Chelsea boots and a blue trilby hat. They were hugely excited and I got quite a write-up in the next day's newspapers – such things had rarely been seen in the Deep South of America in the early 1960s.

One thing I rarely dealt with was cash. Everything would be 'taken care of'; indeed usually in our travels we would be guests of the government or of some rich industrialist or other. Many years later, when I was a private individual again, I had this recurrent fear that one day I would say 'Thank you very much' and walk out of a restaurant without paying, because that had been our routine on so many hundreds of occasions all over the world. A habit not easily broken.

Despite the hectic schedule, we always found time (or made time) to visit the places that really mattered, the Grand Canyon, Disneyland, Hollywood, the Colorado ski-centres, and the gambling dens of Las Vegas. Our visits were always brief affairs, although the trip to Las Vegas was not brief enough for me to avoid winning, and then losing, seventy-five dollars. This was something Lord Louis never let me forget, for everything that happened had to be entered in the Tour Diary, and I truly believe that my few minutes at the tables were the only few minutes I had to myself on this entire tour, and these, of course, were in the early hours of the morning when by rights I should have been tucked up in bed.

By the time we reached New York, preparatory to returning home, I was completely worn out, physically and mentally, but, of course, I knew it was coming to an end. Little did I know what was in store for me!

Lord and Lady Louis were due to fly back to London on the inaugural flight of the new BOAC Comet jet. Because this was very much a VIP occasion with limited space, the remaining four of us in the retinue had to return with the American air force servicemen and their families from the Harmen airbase. We took off in a huge USAF Constellation but the tyres blew out on take-off. There was screaming and some panic, but fortunately nobody was seriously hurt. This was to be the first of my five plane crashes in Lord Louis' service, but fortunately no one was hurt in any of them. I would not wish to repeat any of them and I'm certain each one aged me by ten years!

Chapter Four:
Ban-yans and Fans

Very shortly after I returned from North America, I was given my date for joining the Royal Yacht. The powers that be had kept their promise, and I was suitably grateful. So too had been Lord and Lady Louis, who presented me with a fine silver tankard, beautifully inscribed with a facsimile signature and the Mountbatten of Burma cypher. I treasure it to this day. After what seemed like such a short period of time, I said goodbye to Lord and Lady Louis and Broadlands.

The *Britannia* is the most glamorous naval ship afloat, and just freshly commissioned she was looking her best. She has the most distinctive blue enamelled sides in which you can see your reflection and she is always kept in mint condition. She has a huge, mustard-yellow funnel, a glistening white superstructure, her three masts leaning backwards. All in all, she has a beautiful line on her. In the 1950s she was the best Britain could produce and there was – perhaps there still is – nothing to touch her. Certainly she is more dignified than the ostentatious and glitzy private yachts of the international jetsetters.

At the same time *Britannia* has to be a practical ship. She can without too much trouble be converted to a hospital ship manned by the Royal Navy, and she has been used in that capacity on many naval exercises, most recently in the evacuation of British civilians off-shore from Aden. She carries at all times a surgeon and complete operating theatre, which is used to this day for emergency operations on seamen from other ships mid-ocean.

Her principal disadvantage is that, with so much space

being given over to the royal accommodation, there is considerably less space than would be ideal in the crew's quarters. A lot of thought was given by her designers to the problem of privacy for the Royal Family, and the solution was to build her with the whole of the stern of the vessel almost entirely separate from the rest. You could indeed sail in the crew's quarters without even knowing that you had royals on board. Later on, I had the pleasure of travelling on the Royal Yacht as a member of the entourage. It was just a single night, from Cowes to Milford Haven, where we were to disembark to fly to Ireland and Classiebawn. For me it was like coming home, although my cabin in the royal apartments was considerably more comfortable than the petty officers' mess up forward.

The *Britannia* carried a big complement of sailors. There were some two hundred full-time crew and, when there were royals on board, an extra eighty officers, chefs, stewards, signalmen and so on came on board for Royal Duty.

Even since the *Britannia* came into service there have been sniping criticisms about her as an expensive and outmoded extravagance. But how do you compute such things? On one journey, that yacht can earn export orders for this country worth ten, even twenty times what she has cost. When *Britannia* drops anchor in a foreign port, the local businessmen congregate on board. There is no need to coax or cajole them; they are enchanted to come aboard. They are sometimes treated to a short cruise; they are always entertained regally. The heads of British industries are there to encourage them, and they cheerfully put their signatures to massive import/ export deals. So when the talk is of value, it is important to keep things in perspective, to remember that what we are dealing with is less than the cost of tranquillisers given away annually through the National Health Service. The funds raised by the royals for our country is truly incalculable and the prestige gained the envy of the world. Does the *Britannia* give good value for money? Of course she does!

So there I was in my prime at twenty-seven years old, a petty officer enjoying the best of health and firmly ensconced on the most prestigious vessel in the world with a great company of men. What more could one possible ask for? But to fill my cup of happiness to the brim, my first voyage was to be with Princess Mary, the Princess Royal and the late King's sister, and our destination was my beloved Caribbean, where the Princess would fulfil her duties as Chancellor of the University of the West Indies with a full programme of official visits.

As we ploughed across the Atlantic, I became attuned to the yacht's unique movement; leaping like a leopard from wave to wave. We passed the crazy flying fish and the gregarious dolphins and travelled on through the Sargasso Sea, where eels abound in all their insinuating variety, to Trinidad and Tobago. The further we sailed, the finer the weather became. I had thought that the islands I had already seen would be impossible to better, but at that time Tobago really was *the* Robinson Crusoe island that all castaways dream of. Almost unbelievable.

We worked hard and we deserved something special in the way of relaxation. Accordingly, as the Divisional Petty Officer, I arranged an outing. We loaded a pinnace with a huge canvas tarpaulin, football and cricket gear, Scuba masks, sausages, cans of beer and what in the Navy are called 'tiddly oggies' (Cornish pasties) and sailed off like a pirate crew, landing on a remote beach of the softest powdery pink sand. The sea was pure and translucent as a diamond. Between the palm trees in which parakeets and humming birds swooped and skimmed we spread our tarpaulin for shade. No doubt we would have appeared to an onlooker like a lost tribe of Bedouin, but we were carefree as we set about our unforgettable ban-yan (beach barbecue). Although we would have liked the company of a bunch of pretty girls, it remains in my memory as an unforgettable day, blissful and carefree. No wonder we were late getting back on board.

In Trinidad the MCC touring cricket team including such stalwarts as Freddie Trueman and Alan Laker came on board to a reception. Fiery Fred was on his very best behaviour. Wherever we went, all the expatriates would contact us and come on board. We would drop anchor, receive whoever there was to be received, give them all a dinner, and sail off again before midnight. There was no hanging about. Despite the agreeable surroundings and the occasional ban-yan it was not entirely a holiday cruise for any of us. It was during this journey that I heard the sad news of the death of Lady Mountbatten in Borneo.

Jamaica was the only island on which we enjoyed a prolonged stay. The Princess left the yacht for a few days, which gave us an opportunity to go up country – we had been invited to a party on one of the banana plantations in the Blue Mountains. What we did not know was that the coach which had been laid on for us was also supposed to take the officers still on the yacht to a state banquet in Kingston Town Hall later on. We enjoyed our swim, the delicious tea laid out for us in the colonial-style residence, and the music from a steel band, but when we boarded the coach we were not, as we expected, returned to the yacht, but transported to a big old barn on the plantation which had been cleared and decorated with flags, where the West Indian equivalent of a barn dance was in full swing with the entire workforce and their families.

Meanwhile, the officers kicked their heels and waited for the coach which never came to take them off for their big night out. When we returned on board at about four in the morning, we were not hugely popular. By then, I'm ashamed to say, most of our party were so hopelessly drunk that the officers would not have been able to get their own back on us even if they had threatened to hang us all for mutiny.

From Jamaica we travelled through a treacherous storm across the Gulf of Mexico to Belize, and on to the Great Cayman Islands, where if you leaned over the side of the yacht you could clearly see the giant turtles keeping us company as we approached our anchorage. Then, setting a course between Dominica and Cuba, we headed back to Portsmouth.

During this last stage, in March 1960, I received a summons to FORY otherwise known as the Flag Officer Royal Yachts, a rear admiral. I experienced the same grip of anxiety as at the barracks and ran over in my mind all the crimes of which I fancied I might have been guilty. The news was even worse than I had feared.

'Petty Officer,' said the Rear Admiral, 'I'm sad to tell you that you've got to leave us. Lord Mountbatten has apparently asked for your services permanently to head his retinue.'

(After the death of Lady Louis, Lord Mountbatten had set up a new staff of naval retinue in lieu of the civilian staff which they had previously had in London at Wilton Crescent; he wanted me to head them.)

I was not just dumbfounded and angry, I was heartbroken. I had settled down into the routine of the Royal Yacht Service and I was sublimely happy. I had no further anxieties about my future career. And now this! I had had a taste of life with Mountbatten and I knew how hectic and pressured it was. I dreaded living out of suitcases again.

I told him I could not go. I explained about the promise that had been made to me.

'Of course we're very sad to lose you, but there's really nothing we can do about it.'

'Well, surely,' I said, 'Her Majesty has got to approve my release from the Yacht Service.'

'She already has done.'

There was nothing more to be said. I had a pretty sad crossing, deeply apprehensive of what lay ahead.

Looking back on that summons to the Admiral's cabin which seemed to me at the time so catastrophic, I realise that I was most upset to be missing all the exotic ports of call at which the Royal Yacht would be docking over the years. I need not have worried. In my time with Mountbatten I was to see far more exotic sights, and visit far more remarkable places, than the Yacht ever could or did.

Before I returned to Mountbatten's service on a permanent basis in his naval retinue, however, I was asked, in January 1960, to return to Broadlands on a private understanding that I should help out with the arrangements for the wedding of Lady Pamela, the Mountbattens' younger daughter, to David Hicks. I was happy to do so, as I had, during the short but hectic time of our Canadian tour, grown extremely fond of Edwina, Lady Mountbatten, and the entire Mountbatten family.

The day of the wedding, 13 January, was bitterly cold with the first snow of the year. Broadlands was buzzing with one of the greatest gatherings of the post-war years. With the exception of the pregnant Queen – Prince Andrew was about to appear – just about the whole of society was there. The flurrying snow, which added such a magical charm and fairytale setting to the whole grand affair, kept me busy with a large, stiff broom trying to keep the front door entrance clear in between incessant arrivals. Prince Philip with the very young short-trousered Prince Charles drove up just as I was trying to hide the broom behind the portico pillars. This was my first meeting with our future king. He was extremely shy and we shook hands formally. Princess Anne was one of the bridesmaids. (Lady Pamela herself had been bridesmaid to the Queen and Pamela's daughter, India, would be a bridesmaid at Prince Charles' wedding.)

Lord Louis was everywhere, of course, as the caterers lit huge candelabras for the magnificent banquet tables.

'Surely you don't need these,' he said. 'There are plenty of electric chandeliers.'

No sooner were the words out of his mouth than a massive power cut plunged us all into complete darkness and the caterer's candles were the only illuminations left to us.

One thing I noticed as the lights failed was the Duke of Edinburgh nipping away up the grand staircase for a few minutes' peace. It may be lively and hilarious when all the royals are gathered together, but it is sure to be exhausting as well.

As the endless carloads of close and distant relations arrived, one of the biggest limousines contained an old, smartly dressed lady wrapped in furs whom neither Charles Smith, the butler, nor I was able to identify from our lists. None the less, she announced herself as Princess Victoria of Hildenbergh – or some such odd name – and, although she was not on our list, we bowed politely. Then Charles gave me the nod and I dashed off for Lady Louis.

'There's this old lady in the hall,' I said. 'She claims to be Princess Victoria of Something or Other. I don't know her, Charles doesn't know her; perhaps you do?'

In the hall Lady Louis immediately took charge, kissing the old lady on the cheek and saying: 'My dear, how lovely to see you.' But we had a secret signal, and Lady Louis gave me the wink to indicate that we had a nutcase on the premises, so I left immediately to phone for the police. But not before I heard Lady Louis saying: 'You must be very tired after your journey, Your Royal Highness. Let me take you to your room to tidy up.'

So, on the morning of her daughter's wedding, when we were running to a very tight schedule, she put everything aside just for a while, calmed the old dear, took her to her bedroom, let her wash her hands and sit quietly at her dressing table. Then, when the police were ready, she said: 'Now, dear, these lovely gentlemen are going to take you to your car and we'll see you later.' The old dear went off blissfully happy with her police escort.

Lady Louis had always told her staff to show the greatest compassion to unbalanced people; if you show them up, they are far more likely to do something really silly, like hurling bricks through the car windscreen or committing suicide.

I learned the lesson well, and put it into practice, when I was looking after Lord Louis in London. There we enjoyed the attentions of a regular bunch, and even opened a file on our nutcases. The most memorable was a youngish woman who claimed to be an Austrian countess, and who, like so many women, had a mad crush on my employer. Several times a week she would come calling and ring the bell and I always instructed my boys to take the letter she would have written for Lord Louis and fob her off kindly with some invented story. One day, a new, young steward was peremptory with her and slammed the door in her face. When I got to hear about it, I was furious with him; that evening we read in the paper that she had thrown herself off a roof and killed herself. There was a photograph of her, and the caption said that she *was* an Austrian countess. It put a chill through me, and it made me realise just how right Lady Louis had been to be so compassionate to these unfortunate people who figured so frequently in our lives.

Another of our London regulars was the Cockney, Miss Day, who was four foot nothing, about eighty years old, with a large wart on her nose. She never missed a day. One time after the door was shut in her face, she waited for the postman to call. She knew that since there was nearly always something to be signed for he would ring the bell. As soon as the door was opened, she came flying at me with a heavy wedge of wood. I got the postman inside just in time to avoid serious injury, but I had to let the poor man out of the back door as Miss Day was hanging around for the rest of the morning.

Yet another young woman was in the habit of lying down in front of our car. One way and another we had to be both tactful and careful. We had to try to frighten them off and at the same time to protect them. Several of these women were under the impression that they were Mountbatten's wife, and would demand that he sent a car to collect them. They were packed, they insisted, and ready to join him. There were other letters containing the most intimate fantasies. He would read these letters in bed in the morning and, if there was a really fruity one, he would sling it at me, saying: 'Evans, I think this must be for you. I don't even know the woman.'

In view of what was to happen, we were well advised to be security-conscious, and in the era of letter bombs we were particularly suspicious of unidentified parcels. One such was left on the doorstep late one night, and we got the police to look at it. As soon as it was touched, it emitted a most sinister whirring noise; this was one for the experts of the bomb squad. Their delicate instruments pried and prodded to reveal an expensive toy, a double-decker tin bus left by an unknown admirer for Princess Alexandra's first baby, imminently expected.

Generally, Lord Louis enjoyed opening his own letters, in part because he loved using the gadget the young Prince Charles had given him as a Christmas present, a small black box which magically opened letters on command. It was an intelligent present. Lord Louis loved all gadgets and was never happier than when investigating the whys and wherefores of machinery.

When letters from nuts arrived, I was always instructed to take very good care that cries for help from pensioners trying to get their war pensions were put to one side. Lord Louis always helped when he could, and followed up each case to make sure that necessary action had been taken. There were also endless requests from charities throughout the world, particularly scouting and ex-service organisations, for items which could be sold to raise funds. We quickly ran out of caps, buttons and epaulettes and were reduced to old uniform lace from the sleeve ranks; then these too became scarce and from sending a full ring of gold lace, it became no more than an inch or two. I'm glad to say, however, that we always managed something, although it did become an increasingly difficult task as well as a pretty time-consuming and costly affair. Rarely did a day pass without requests for autographs, books or photographs, and Lord Louis did his best to please everyone, though it certainly added to my work load because I was landed with most of it.

Shortly after the joyousness of Lady Pamela's wedding, great sadness followed. Lady Louis went off to the Far East on a more than usually demanding tour on behalf of the St John's Ambulance Brigade and the Save the Children Fund, for whom she was such a tireless president. She had been in poor health with a mild jaundice before the wedding, and, although both family and doctors begged her not to go, she would not hear of abandoning the tour. From the snows of England she went straight to the tropical humidity of the jungles of Borneo. Here in the past she had insisted that a medical team be sent in to organise immunisation jabs for the native children, and had refused to leave until it was confirmed that a team was on its way. But on this occasion it was her own health which was at risk.

The Almighty took her into His keeping while she was asleep in a small bare wooden house on a hill at Jesselton, surrounded by the poor people she had worked so hard to help. Out of love for her sailor husband she asked to be buried at sea, as a tribute to him; and so she was, with an escort willingly provided by the Indian Navy and the Royal Navy.

It was so fitting an end to such a fine lady, one who had possessed great beauty, great compassion, great wealth, a wonderful family, yet spent and gave so much of her life to those less fortunate.

Only the drifting wreaths cast into the ocean by her devastated husband and Prince Philip, her nephew, marked the final resting place of this lady. The world was a better place for her gifts to it, and a much sadder one for her passing.

Today, Lord Louis lies in Romsey Abbey, where Lady Pamela and David Hicks were married.

The first tour I undertook as an official member of Lord Louis' retinue was to Kenya, Uganda, Southern Rhodesia and Zanzibar in the autumn of 1960. It may have been because I was new to such delights, but it seems to me to have been one of the most enchanting tours we undertook.

Most of our travelling was done on our own aircraft, an RAF Comet specially fitted out for us, and it became our second home. Up front was a small sleeping cabin and a wardrobe room. Next came a conference room where a clutch of C-in-Cs or ambassadors could hold meetings between stops. Then there was the 'office', for the ADCs and the girl stenographers from the Ministry of Defence and their flying fingers. At the rear of the plane would be space for service personnel and sometimes their families, because it must be remembered that most of our routes (Aden to Singapore to Hong Kong to Manila, etc.) would cover the regular military staging posts.

The RAF were fantastic. If the programme said 'Arrive Kuala Lumpur at 1710 local', we would open the doors at precisely that time. And if we sometimes used local companies, and anything from helicopters to hovercraft, it was always a joy to rejoin our beloved (and air-conditioned) RAF once more. There were no idle moments. We would work together on speeches: he would learn them, then relate them to me whilst I checked him on details – I must say he was pretty good and rarely made mistakes. Then he would sign the endless flow of letters and signals, eat and, just occasionally, sleep in mid-air.

But that first tour did permit us to enjoy many of the glories of Africa. We were state guests at the Governor-General's house in Nairobi, where there were huge receptions and garden parties for three thousand people. Then we flew off in little planes to the Royal Lodge, Sagana, a charming thatched cottage. Set amongst masses of gloriously coloured bougainvillea bushes, it looked down across the vast African plains, shimmering with the heat, to the snow-capped heights of Mount Kilimanjaro. Sagana had been a wedding present to

Princess Elizabeth from the peoples of Africa. The first thing to be pointed out to us when we arrived were the recent bullet-holes around the front door from a Mau Mau attack, but mercifully they had not chosen to burn it down as they had the original Treetops. However, we had an army escort guarding the place at all times. (The Queen returned Sagana to the people when the new state gained its independence.)

In the course of a quick safari around the game park, we saw a pride of lions with their babies; we saw a huge python lying in a hole where it had been for three weeks digesting a gazelle, part of which was still sticking out of its mouth. It would live on that gazelle, we were told, for nine months or so. As we drove along in the Land-rover, ostriches would lope alongside us and warthogs scuttle in front of us the way rabbits do in English country lanes. There were giraffe, wildebeeste, buffalo. Secretary birds perched on the backs of the larger mammals, pecking at delicious morsels of flea. Lord Louis, a fanatical photographer, like all the Royal Family, used reel upon reel of cine film.

During our all too short visit to Sagana, I had hung Lord Louis' magnificent white Tropical Naval Tunic on the door of a wardrobe to shake out the creases which packing inevitably produced. Upon returning from our safari, I was horrified to see this Full Dress Uniform floating in a tin laundry bowl over a fire in the yard, with William, a lanky, toothless laundry boy from Government House in Nairobi poking at it with a stick. That, I instinctively felt, was the end of that uniform, but worse was to follow when I saw William stuffing smouldering charcoal into a huge old iron. There was nothing to be done but to curse my fate. A while later, however, that uniform was returned to me whiter and more immaculate than I had ever seen it, and perfectly ironed (a difficult job considering the complications of padded shoulders and such); a result better than was ever achieved by our highly professional London launderers.

From Sagana we travelled to Treetops, which is in the very heart of the bush. It lives up to its name, since it is built on wooden stilts perched in the trees. You can only approach it by foot, and you may only take with you the minimum of personal effects in a night bag. Nothing scented is permitted, no aerosols or soaps, no perfumes or hair sprays, as the wild animals would come nowhere near otherwise. It was while staying in the original rather more primitive Treetops Hotel that Princess Elizabeth and Prince Philip received the drastic news of the King's death, and it is almost accurate to say that the Queen ascended the throne of England while 'up a gum tree'. A plaque marks the site.

As we were escorted along the jungle path by armed rangers, we passed these huge nuts on the ground about the size of avocado pears. Lord Louis asked what they were, and it was explained to him that they were nuts from a kind of fruit which had passed through the elephants' digestive systems as a highly efficient laxative. Lord Louis instructed me to find ten of them, explaining that they would be perfect for the children's Christmas stockings.

'I know where they've been,' I said in mock disgust. So he picked one up himself and I had no option but to pick up the rest.

We were also puzzled by small stockades in which were poles sticking out of the ground with horizontal treads on them, like miniature telegraph poles.

'What on earth are they for?' Lord Louis wanted to know, and it was explained that they were escape poles in the event of being charged by wild rhino. You cannot hear them, and if they see you or smell you, they put their heads down and charge. At once he said: 'Come on, Evans, up you go.' (It always had to be me, of course.) 'Come on, test it out; there's a charging rhino after you.'

His voice had taken on a convincingly urgent tone and I ran like an idiot up the pole, playing to the gallery on command as usual, while the rest of the party collapsed with laughter. The pole, which was rotten, gave way and I fell off it, through a fence and into some bushes on which I scratched myself extremely painfully all over. They continued to bellow with laughter while I lay upside down in this bloody bush and Lord Louis announced: 'Hard luck, Evans, now you're a rhino's breakfast, ha-ha!' I was not amused.

Eventually, we reached Treetops, my pride smarting as much as my body, and we climbed up ladders to the verandah, which was high above the trees and overlooking a dirty-

The evacuees at the vicarage: the brothers Mulvaner and myself (facing)

The eight-year-old author

My war refuge, Helperthorpe Vicarage

My first bicycle. It took me three years to save the £18 for this.

My first ship. Hall-boy at Knapton Hall.

The petty officers of the Royal Yacht *Britannia*, 1960, on my first and only royal cruise through the Caribbean. I'm seated front row, far left.

In New Zealand on my first world tour with Mountbatten, 1961. Chief Petty Officer Jack Nelson, Lord Louis' PA, is seated far left. I am the second on the right.

At the Borneo war front, 1963. Sir Solly Zuckermann is just visible, seated behind, without a cap. Lord Louis is seated front right.

En route to Nehru's funeral. I am on the far left and David Divine of the *Sunday Times* is fifth from the right.

Lord Mountbatten the bird of paradise, with Lady Patricia behind him, New Guinea, 1965

Australia, 1965 – I'm the cuddly one

My prized swordfish. New Zealand second time round, Otehei Bay, 1965.

'Alloa' from Moorea, Tahiti, halfway round the world, 1965

The castaway off Tahiti, 1965

The presidential palace, Monrovia, 1964: what Prince Charles would call a carbuncle

Lining up to lead a Mexican rodeo, Lord Mountbatten is in his element surrounded by beautiful girls and magnificent horses

looking watering-hole. Here we were served with thick chunks of juicy, fresh pineapple on forks. I was chatting to Mr Sherbrook Walker, an old African explorer of about seventy with a fine white beard, when I felt my hand yanked away and there on the fence was an enormous baboon scoffing my piece of pineapple. I was furious because I was very hot and thirsty and after my recent exertions it had been more than usually welcome. Snatching food is, I learnt, a favourite trick of these Kenyan baboons, and you should not protest too vigorously. They are quite wild and would tear your eyes out as soon as look at you. None the less, I was furious and told this baboon off in no uncertain terms.

Dusk falls suddenly in Africa and no sooner had we settled in than it was dark. The Treetops water-hole is provided with an ingenious system of artificial moonlight. You sit around the hole, sixty feet below you, on an old airline seat under a rug, and wait. While we were waiting, dinner interrupted our curfew. It was a formal meal with a printed menu, thus:

> Potage Mount Kenya
>
> Asperges au beurre
>
> Treetops Pie
> Pommes de terre au four
> Légumes de saison
>
> Pêches flambées
>
> Café
> (locally grown Wahenya Estate)

As far as the Treetops Pie was concerned, I dreaded to think what might have been in it, though it looked like an innocuous steak pie. We had just started on it when we were asked to be quiet and we tiptoed to the verandah from where we could see a herd of about fifty elephants. Their approach had been entirely silent. The rangers had laid salt for them days previously and this had lured them to the watering-hole so their arrival was not entirely fortuitous. We were guaranteed a good show.

As the early evening progressed, we saw lovely little gazelles, small deer, then warthogs with their secretary birds. The elephants who had stayed for a couple of hours, drinking and licking the salt, moved on puffing and blowing. After a long break, the buffalo came in, and a little after midnight two huge white rhino arrived, who had the water-hole entirely to themselves.

With so much to watch, we were naturally reluctant to leave. When I finally got to my room it was to sleep in a bed with the big bough of a tree growing right across it. However, the bed itself was covered with elegant white linen and the branches of the tree were handsomely padded so that one did oneself no injury during the night.

From Treetops we moved on to the Victoria Falls and stood on the very spot where Livingstone is reputed to have shaken hands with Dr Stanley. The falls seemed thrilling enough to me, but we were told that the water pressure was low and could be four or five times more powerful than it was during our visit. It was an impressive sight all the same.

We took a twenty-foot narrow boat along the Zambesi River, passing elephants and giraffes, all sorts of gazelles and snakes, until we encountered a group of enormous snorting hippos. Disliking the heat of the sun, these creatures remain submerged with only their little piggy ears and eyes visible above the surface of the water. As the boat approached the hippos, Lord Louis decided that he must photograph them. As we nudged towards them, a big old bull became aggressive and reared up, his great jaws open wide, some three feet across. Thrilled, Lord Louis kept inching towards the front of the boat, cine camera loaded, myself close behind him with the second camera, but a little apprehensive as we were no more than a yard above the beast's mouth.

'My God, look at that, look at that,' he cried, pointing the zoom directly down those giant jaws. He seemed oblivious of the danger.

Everyone inched forward until the boat started taking water, and still he filmed. Lord Louis, at sixty-five, was not a young man, so, I, becoming increasingly concerned, grabbed hold of his bush shirt. Had I not done so, I am convinced that he would have been lunch for the hippos that day.

A little later one of the ladies in our party decided to change from her tiny shorts into something a little more presentable before we landed. Lord Louis gallantly shielded her from sight while she struggled out of the shorts and into slacks, but the zip stuck. Lord Louis came to the rescue, but tug and pull as he might the zip remained jammed. In desperation he turned to me: 'Evans will do it. Come on, Evans.'

I knew about zips. All I had to do was go back one notch and it instantly freed itself.

Everyone looked on in amazement, and Lord Louis cried: 'What can you do with this bloody man? Can he never fail?' At the same time he squeezed his hands together in a characteristic gesture of delight.

Our next port of call was Salisbury, where we were to stay with Sir Roy Welensky, the Prime Minister. It was here that for the only time in my career I disgraced myself by getting lost, though it was not entirely my fault.

Lord Louis was taken directly from the airport to a meeting with the Prime Minister and the tribal chiefs, while I took the luggage in a separate car to the residence. At least the residence was where I believed myself to be going, but after twenty minutes of what was supposed to be a ten-minute trip I realised that we were leaving the city behind and concluded that I was being kidnapped.

'Stop, stop, go back,' I cried.

The explanation was less sinister than I had feared. My driver, an African soldier who spoke not a word of English, had been heading for Chequers, the Prime Minister's country house outside the city, instead of his beautiful bungalow in Salisbury.

After Lord Louis heard about this, he insisted that I was with him at all times. On one occasion, we were travelling in two small eight-seater USAF aeroplanes, Lord Louis with the American four-star generals and I with the aides-de-camp and equerries. As soon as he realised what was happening, Lord Louis said to one of the generals, 'Would you mind going in the other plane? I need Evans with me,' and with that he turfed him out. Lord Louis could not take the risk of not having me and my little bag of tricks to hand. As he said: 'Evans is the man I rely on, and I don't want him lost like he was in Salisbury. Four-star generals are no use to me, it's Evans I need. He keeps me straight on everything.'

It was not unusual for the second aircraft to land maybe half an hour after Lord Louis' plane, by which time he was quite likely to need a change of uniform and endless things that I had to carry, like gifts and speech folders. It was no use my being some five hundred miles away! He needed his personal chap at hand at *all* times. Lord Louis was always so practical.

After Salisbury we enjoyed a quick tour of Bulawayo, visiting the magnificent new Kariba Dam. The political situation did not permit us to enter South Africa but we did see Nyasaland and the Zomba Plateau. This is a fascinating place with jacaranda trees as far as the eye can see on a raised flat-topped plateau. Nearly every colour in the paint box is there – blues, yellows, greens, reds, orangey-whites and purples – and the scents are overwhelming. You would have thought that Walt Disney had gone along with his brush half an hour before we arrived and painted it. And in the background above the shimmering heat of the desert plains is the familiar but endlessly exciting backcloth of Mount Kilimanjaro with its snowy cap.

These tours, which were to become regular features of my life for the next ten years, were organised by the Ministry of Defence. Six to nine months before the start of a major tour I would receive my first draft. This would be extremely vague, merely announcing: 'Arrive Hong Kong . . . leave Hong Kong . . . arrive Malaya . . . leave Malaya . . .' I would take little notice of either this or of the second, third, fourth or fifth drafts, which would be extensively added to and amended. I would wait for the sixth draft, by which time it would contain three pages of detailed requirements for Hong Kong; with that to hand I would begin to work out everything that Lord Louis would need for that stop-over.

If it was a world tour, I would receive anything up to twelve drafts, which would have been regularly updated, and then, after discussions with the ADC, I would get right down to my vital part in the enterprise.

My biggest headache was trying to work out all the climatic

changes we would encounter. If the tour was extensive enough, we would have to take the entire wardrobe. In the early tours for which I was responsible, Lord Louis had not yet been created Colonel of the Lifeguards or Colonel Commandant Royal Marines, so we were only concerned with naval uniforms. Later, things became hellishly complicated.

I would study the drafts and create my own lists from them, often working late into the night. When we would need full dress tropical whites, when we would need khaki bush jackets and so on. I knew that whenever possible Lord Louis would want to get out of uniform, and I had to be ready for countless instant changes for polo, fishing and riding.

To simplify things, I devised a luggage system which appeared not unlike a treble-chance pools coupon. Down the left-hand side of my chart was a column marking every piece of luggage – some eighty pieces. The first half-dozen were regular travelling cases with all the basic requirements which I knew we would need throughout the tour. If we were going straight to the Far East, the next cases on the list would contain tropical kit and equipment, and so on. I had to include clothes for formal evening engagements, white dinner jackets for embassies, full evening uniform dress for pompous government-house dos. The most pompous were the formal functions hosted by the governor-generals of New Zealand and Australia, which were far more grand than anything in our own royal palaces. The governor's lady and the ambassador's wife would often be so thorough that I would be pulled up by the ADC with a message like: 'His Excellency asks would you please make sure you are wearing your jacket when you cross the landing.' But Lord Louis' attitude was always: 'Take your jackets off and roll your sleeves up', which was the only sensible thing to do in the sort of temperatures we often encountered. I couldn't please everyone all the time, but it was essential to be as diplomatic as possible and avoid offending our hosts.

The volume of packing was formidable, but I knew that the most important items would be my stand-by cases. Packing is an art, and one which, after so much experience, I believe I have mastered. I would challenge anyone to pack military uniforms as quickly and efficiently as I did. I even came to enjoy it. I would have stand-bys of absolutely everything, and I learnt fast.

In those days when you took to the air your fountain pens, which did not take kindly to decompression, would leak. All official Ministry business would have to be done in green ink, and all private papers in black. So I needed a quantity of spares and I had to watch out that all pens were removed from uniforms before take-off.

My greatest friend on all the trips was what became known as the Fairbanks Case. This was a handsome, tall pigskin travelling case which Douglas Fairbanks Jnr had presented to Lord Louis for Christmas. It had three adjustable sections which were, I suppose, intended for shirts. Its first enormous advantage was that it always remained upright, the handle on top, and I learned to remove all fountain pens from breast pockets to a cigar case lined with blotting paper, which was then placed inside the Fairbanks. It also contained photographs and photo frames, and envelopes to protect the unframed photographs to be given to those who were not grand enough for framed ones. A few in very special silver frames were to be dished out to very high-ranking monarchs and princes, who might also receive silver-gilt cufflinks in presentation boxes. There was also a miscellany of gifts for unforeseen occasions – ashtrays with the Mountbatten of Burma cypher, silver cigarette boxes engraved with facsimile signatures and soon on. In the case was extra film for the cine camera and every possible kind of pill and tablet – these would purify water, settle tummies, avoid sunburn, give salt, repel insects and, if those failed, ease insect bites. There were plasters for minor injuries and bandages for more serious ones. There were boxes of loo paper and refreshing tissues. There was official headed stationery and private headed stationery. There were spare specklets (small folding spectacles) and index cards for speech notes. There were cordless electric razors with the batteries fully charged and spare socks and pants; boiled sweets and peppermints; decorations, sashes, medals, ties and badges as appropriate – all duplicates; sunglasses, sunhats and small cigars in tin-foil containers.

I blessed Douglas Fairbanks every day for this wonderful,

wonderful case, which served me faithfully all those years.

I believe that I can honestly say that during the ten years of my working life with Lord Louis I never once failed him, although there were plenty of times when I might have done.

For example, on one occasion, the programme stipulated: 'Arrive in Bangkok – Undress Tropical White Number 5 Naval Day Uniform', but when our plane taxied to a halt we could see all the bigwigs lined up with their glittering medals and their imposing sashes; there were banners flying, guard of honour cannons booming, the whole shebang. This was formal all right, and the King's Chamberlain was wearing the sash of the Siamese Order of the White Elephant, which is a stunning sash with a rainbow pattern of colours from maroon to scarlet to gold and so on.

Although it had not been specified, I had one standing by on top of my magic case, so that when Mountbatten looked out of the window and said: 'Good God, they're wearing sashes,' and started to panic, I could immediately respond with: 'All right, all right, I've got it here.'

Once he was in his sash he relaxed enough to grin at me and say so that everyone in the aircraft could hear: 'Can we never catch him out?'

They never did, though I was often tested to the limit.

The art lay in anticipating what *could* happen, because, if it could, you might be sure that one day it would. And it did.

No. He never did catch me out.

Lord Louis left all the packing and the preparations entirely to me. The only time I can remember him interesting himself in the arrangements was once when, just before a major tour, he remarked: 'You are packing a few spare films, aren't you, Evans? Pack a dozen.' I had already packed six dozen, although I was not about to tell him that. Once, he came into the room when I was in the throes of packing and saw a heap of films and snorted: 'That's ridiculous. You don't need half of those. Send them back; I only need a dozen.' So I packed three dozen, and had to signal for the rest before the tour was halfway through. After that, I tended to ignore any instructions from him and packed exactly what I had worked out we might need. In those days, these small cine films were not available throughout the world – certainly never in the middle of the African bush.

Frequently we would be in the wilds somewhere and he would demand a new colour film roll for his 8mm cine camera, although 'officially' we had used up our supply of film some two weeks earlier. Then I might remind him that had it not been for me, etc., etc., and he would give me a rather mischievous grin, biff me on the shoulder and ask me what did I think I was doing there anyway and why on earth did I think he had chosen me for the job? Whereupon I would whistle a snatch of the hornpipe which he understood to mean that I was enjoying every minute of it, and we would exchange smiles. When Lord Louis smiled, it was his way of emphasising just how much he depended on me.

We were great friends and came to understand each other pretty well, although never once did I overstep my position. I always treated him with the polite courtesy appropriate for a Chief Petty Officer with his Admiral.

Ironically, never once, to my knowledge, did any of us, Lord Louis included, get a chance to view a single inch of all those miles of footage he shot on our numerous tours.

Packing for a world tour was one problem. Another, and potentially a more serious one, was getting everything home, because we would be given so many and such impractical gifts, and would usually end up with more than we started with. On our last trip to Africa, in 1965, the Prime Minister of Nigeria gave us a lizard, a gekko I think it was, a little beauty.

Lord Louis said: 'What shall we call it? We'll have to have a name for it.' So we all racked our brains and I suggested that since the Prime Minister had given the animal to us we ought to call it after the Prime Minister. So we called it Abbubarker. On the way home it got loose in the aircraft, but we tracked it down in the end. The sad thing was that shortly after we reached home we heard that the Prime Minister had been murdered by rebels. The lizard outlasted him by years and lived happily enough at Broadlands. The only complication was that we had to breed maggots for it as its staple diet was flies which it 'shot' with its enormously long tongue.

In Peru the Incas presented us with what appeared to be a large and finely wrought pole. It was too long to fit in any of the cases and was decorated with pretty ribbons and bows and all sorts of dangly things. Well, at Lima railway station I was carrying it (since I could not fit it into any of the cases) when the entire station fell instantly to its knees. I was flummoxed. What was happening? Was I supposed to go down on my knees too? Then an old man came forward and grovelled before me and kissed the pole. It seemed that they thought I was an Inca chief, perhaps even a god. I felt most ridiculous and managed to escape into an office doorway, taking the pole with me, whilst everyone was busy grovelling.

I took care after that to ensure that I got the thing wrapped up when travelling amongst the people of Peru, as I did with any other tribal gift – just in case.

Often Lord Louis would be asked what presents he would like. Frequently he would be given items of native dress, such as a rug-cape of many colours given to him by an Ashanti king, or a complete gaucho's outfit presented to him once in South America. This consisted of a Mexican cloak and hood, a short grey jacket with silver buttons linked by a silver chain, huge spurs, a gigantic sombrero laced with silver, a boot-lace tie, a magnificent hide belt with an engraved silver buckle, a silk shirt and tight jodhpurs. This rig he was to wear at the head of a parade in which I must say, surrounded by beautiful local girls mounted sidesaddle and wearing long and colourful dresses, he looked terrific.

In Burma Lord Louis was given the Burmese national costume, a collarless blouse, a loose skirt and flip-flops. Even in this eccentric outfit he looked great, towering over the Burmese and ramrod stiff as always at a national dinner in Rangoon. I recall that he gave a piece of Thai silk to Queen Louise of Sweden, who said she would have it made up into ties for the King; clearly she thought it was *tie* silk!

In the South Seas once, I bought myself a rather snazzy beach shirt and shorts. When Lord Louis saw them he immediately said – and most indignantly: 'Where's mine?' and then: 'Well, why haven't you bought me one?' which I set about doing post haste. After which we both wore them whenever we had a rare opportunity to relax in such places as Nassau and Acapulco.

We were given plaques from regiments and ships, daggers from sheikhs, totem poles from Red Indians, paintings, books and carvings, photographs of self-important dignitaries, models of junks, ivory knickknacks, fishing tackle and military caps. The generous and various supply seemed endless. Even a crate of fresh mangoes from General Ne Win, the President of Burma.

Some of the presents Lord Louis was given we handed over to the British School in the country we were visiting, but there would be some which would be too precious, such as Eskimo stone carvings (increasingly rare), a magnificent jewel-studded dagger given to him by the Sultan and Emirs of Bahrain, and – equally precious to those who gave it to him – some rather doubtful-looking pickaxes from the poorest Indians of New Guinea. Gifts of especial interest were absorbed into the 'Living Museum' collection now on public display at Broadlands. I would have to be able to produce any or all of these at a moment's notice, should we be visited at Broadlands by that country's prime minister, president or monarch.

The most formidable items in this museum were the Japanese guns taken by Lord Louis' forces in the recapture of Singapore; one of them is mounted in the courtyard at Broadlands as a permanent reminder of those stirring events. It struck me as an odd choice, for Mountbatten had the most implacable hatred in his heart for the Japanese and for what many of them did to his men in that war. Even the chaplain of the South-east Asia Command Forces, now the great Bishop Wilson, who used to officiate at the Albert Hall Burma Star Reunions, was tortured. His toenails and fingernails were wrenched out, along with other vile atrocities which he would not divulge, even when his Supreme Commander ordered him to do so. Lord Louis refused for the remainder of his life to have any truck with the Japanese, and one can well imagine what his reaction would have been to Hirohito's funeral.

Once, when he was being briefed about a certain diplomatic dinner, Lord Louis was told, as protocol required, who his neighbours at the top table were to be. As soon as he learnt that he was to be seated next to the wife of the Japanese ambassador, he was extremely upset and let it be known that he would on no account attend the dinner unless the seating arrangements were changed. Nor would he leave for the dinner until he had been assured that the changes had been made. It must have been most embarrassing for his host, but in this matter he was immovable.

It may be that Lord Louis had this Japanese gun set in the courtyard and the second gun in the memorial park of his home town of Romsey as a personal monument to the courage of all the dead heroes who were brutally tortured, to those who suffered in the prisoner-of-war camps, and to those who died in the course of the Burma campaign.

Mountbatten preserved in the Broadlands collection the ceremonial sword – the Japanese instrument of surrender – as well as the document itself and the pens with which it was signed. They have pride of place along with his most treasured possession, the sword which symbolises his Freedom of the City of London and which is always mounted above the Japanese sword as a symbol of superiority. At the time of the surrender he demanded from the Japanese field marshal his second full-dress sword which he handed, on his return to Britain, to the King of England. This was the last ceremony at which a sword was handed over as a symbol of surrender between warring nations.

Each year Mountbatten attended the Great Burma Star reunion at the Royal Albert Hall and the spirit of comradeship was something to be experienced. I would squeeze into the very back of the topmost gallery and would be in tears most of the time as I looked down on so many of these chaps, some limbless, some tortured in mind and body, but all giving a tremendous reception to the singing by Vera Lynn, 'the Forces sweetheart', to the performances by the young servicemen and to the speeches by Field Marshal Lord 'Bill' Slim and Lord Louis. Naturally, I felt something of an intruder between these survivors and their dead companions, but I do hope they will forgive me and feel, as I felt, that I was in my small way representing the rest of us who owe our freedom to men like them.

On such occasions, Lord Louis would conclude his remarks

with a really splendid peroration: 'Normally one wishes organisations to grow from strength to strength but I hope I may not be misunderstood when I say that I hope we may grow less and less, and may God grant that never again we have the need of such wars.'

The old boys would roar with appreciation and give a standing ovation to their two greatest leaders.

Chapter Five:
Wellington Boots and Iced Lollies

Broadlands is a magnificent country house, once the manor house of the Abbey of Romsey. When the abbey was surrendered to Henry VIII, the house passed to the St Barbe family. Much improved during the late seventeenth and early eighteenth centuries, it fell upon hard times when the heir to the estate lost a fortune over the South Sea Bubble. The first Lord Palmerston bought the house and made it 'fit for a gentleman to live in', employing the finest talents. Capability Brown landscaped the garden with the advice of Robert Adam on architectural matters. Henry Holland planned the interiors with Angelica Kauffmann and Josiah Wedgwood. Furniture from France, marble statues from Italy, Canalettos, Van Dykes and Gainsboroughs created, where once Benedictine nuns had prayed and studied on the banks of the trout-rich River Test, a living memorial to all that was best in European taste.

Through the complicated marriages of the great political families of Melbourne, Palmerston and Shaftesbury the house eventually passed to Wilfrid, the only son of Evelyn Ashley. Handsome, respectable, rich and aloof, a political reactionary of the most rigorous kind, Wilfrid chose as his bride Maudie Cassel, a beautiful and talented woman whose father, a Jew who had converted to Catholicism when his dying wife requested it, was one of the wealthiest men in England. Thus Edwina, the elder daughter, inherited Broadlands, and with it the wild estate and Irish Gothic castle of Classiebawn, County Sligo, where her family spent every August.

Edwina was delighted to be invited to stay with her grandfather at Brook House, Park Lane. Here she became his hostess, and here, despite numerous petty restrictions and constraints, she began to spread her wings.

During the early twenties, Edwina, 'the richest heiress in England', became one of the 'fast' set, dancing the Charleston with the other bright young things, amongst whom Miss Barbara Cartland was one of the brightest and one of the youngest. At a ball given at Claridge's in the 1920s by Cornelius Vanderbilt Edwina met a dashingly good-looking young naval lieutenant, and the following year, during Cowes week, the friendship blossomed into love. That naval lieutenant was Lord Louis ('Dickie') Mountbatten.

Shortly afterwards, Edwina Ashley's grandfather died, leaving seven and a half million pounds, of which Edwina was the main beneficiary, although she did not know this when she met her lieutenant. At the time Lord Louis was earning a lieutenant's pay in the Navy. Edwina had to borrow £100 to follow him to India, where he was accompanying the Prince of Wales on his grand tour of the sub-continent. They became engaged in a room at the University of Delhi. At the time, Lady Reading, the Vicereine, said, 'Oh dear, how I wish Edwina was marrying someone with more of a future ahead of him.'

Edwina and Louis were married at St Margaret's, Westminster, on 18 July 1922, with the Prince of Wales as best man and most of the crowned heads of Europe in attendance. They spent their honeymoon touring America in a special train and at Broadlands, where, thirty-seven years later, I was to have my first meeting with the man who was to change and enrich my life.

Lady Louis was a very great lady, an heiress who devoted her life to relieving poverty and suffering. When Lord Louis had been Viceroy of India and she his Vicereine, she had often toured the back streets of Delhi rescuing sick children. Her charitable enterprises were wide-ranging, from the St John's Ambulance Brigade and the Royal College of Nursing to the Girl Guides and the Save the Children Fund, taken over after her death by HRH the Princess Royal.

It is true that the Mountbattens sometimes lived quite separate lives. The diversity of their interests and duties required that they should. But all I ever saw between them was deep love and devotion. Certainly after the death of Edwina, there was no mistaking the anguish Lord Louis clearly felt, and the loneliness that followed. He had always worked hard; for three years after her death he drove himself, and those around him, to the point of exhaustion.

They had separate bedrooms and bathrooms, as indeed do most of the Royal Family and British aristocracy. Practical considerations override personal ones. As for separate dressing-rooms, these are essential. On our first African tour there would be occasions when Lord and Lady Louis shared a double room and there was no dressing-room at all. I was working in the room with Lord Louis while her ladyship was dressing, and nobody turned a hair. While I was organising Lord Louis' change, or buttoning him up, she would shout out: 'Would somebody zip me up?' and over I would trot to become a lady's maid. We became very down to earth about such enforced intimacy, but we all much preferred separate rooms.

Space was essential with the vast amount of luggage we were forced to carry about, and baths were always a problem. When you are in a tropical climate and hot and sticky, a bath becomes an urgent necessity, but three or four minutes was all that was ever allowed on the schedule for both of them to bath. When ignorant people bemoan the fact that the royal and the famous seldom share rooms, they expose their ignorance, not realising just how little time there is, and just how much needs to get done.

We spent as much time at Broadlands as we could, and most week-ends when we were not on tour and Lord Louis could get away from the Ministry of Defence. Occasionally, just to unwind from the great pressures, I would escape for half an hour and jump on one of the big lawn mowers to cut the vast sweeping lawns. Seeing that I had disappeared one day, Lord Louis asked Charles the butler what I was up to. On being told that I had gone out to have a break, he promptly did likewise. So, there we were, both scooting around on these huge mowers – much to the delight of the two overworked gardeners, Reg and Bill!

In any event, I had to do most of my work from Broadlands. Lord Louis' official secretary in London was Vice-Admiral Sir Ronald Brockman, who dealt principally with affairs of state. The private secretary at Broadlands was Commander Ben Webb, who tackled the copious correspondence and handled the estate office and farm matters. When Lord Louis and I left on a major tour, it would usually be from Broadlands where the robes, the decorations, the vast collection of uniforms, and just about everything else we might need was stored. There was certainly no room in the London house for such a vast amount of clobber.

Broadlands was not open to the public until well into the seventies. Before then it was occasionally opened up for charity occasions but was very much a private house where were held the finest house parties anyone could ever wish to attend. The house was not huge. It could comfortably accommodate about eight or ten visitors; but these eight or ten might well include a couple of royals. Since Queen Victoria's offspring had married so extensively into European royalty, most members of the royal houses were also cousins. It was commonplace in a single week-end to be playing host to a variety of kings and queens, princes and princesses, and meeting them unexpectedly on the stairs on in the corridors it was by no means easy to remember who was 'Your Majesty', who 'Your Royal Highness' and who 'Your Serene Highness'.

Lord Louis would do his best to ensure that each week-end was a well-balanced affair. There might be some minor royals, say Princess Alexandra and Angus Ogilvy, along with people from the world of entertainment such as Douglas Fairbanks Jnr and his wife or possibly Maria Callas and Rex Harrison.

There was often a sprinkling of politicians. Harold Macmillan came to us direct from Moscow, still wearing the magnificent white astrakhan hat which had been presented to him there. He had been the first British Prime Minister to visit Moscow since the Revolution, and I remember him saying: 'They showed me the collective farms that they have running there. Show-places, you know. And if that's what they choose to show a British Prime Minister on his first visit, I would hate to think what the rest of the place must be like.'

The most important visitors would sometimes bring their

own staff with them, but Broadlands had a reputation for being such a lovely place to visit, so comfortable and well run that when Lord Louis told his friends: 'You don't have to bring your man, my chap Evans will look after you,' they were usually delighted to leave their own staff at home. And I believe that, of all the hundreds of guests I looked after at Broadlands over the years, there was not one whom I was not delighted to serve.

Charlie Chaplin came to stay. I could not get over it; I could not believe it was possible. That wonderful crazy man, whose antics I had idolised on the screen of the Hull flea-pit cinema so many years ago, had come to stay with us! Though I was to look after him personally I never told him about the cemetery jam jars or the liquorice. I wonder whether he would have been amused.

He was then over eighty and looked like an old English toff. He was white-haired, chubby and small; he wore a beautiful camelhair overcoat, and he walked with a stick, though not his famous cane; he had a bit of a breathing problem but the magic was still there, still that mischievous twinkle in his eye. His delightful wife Oona always accompanied him.

Like most of our guests, he was asked to plant a commemorative tree. The little silver spade was produced which the Royal Family and celebrities from all over the world had always used to plant their trees and Charlie did his bit too. It was a very cold autumn day, and the leaves were off the trees. He took off his overcoat, his scarf and gloves. He walked around the hole, puffing and blowing and shaking his head and treating us to one of his classic comedy routines. He knew, I'm sure, that he wasn't expected to actually plant the thing; the first spadeful of earth would have been enough; but not enough for him. He got out his handkerchief and wiped his brow. He walked around the tree looking meaningfully at it – and it was only a tiny sapling – a bit as weightlifters do before they pick up their weights. He was hyping himself up for the job in hand. Then he rolled his sleeves up, spat on both hands, took hold of the silver spade – and dropped it at once, because of its immense weight. After shovelling each little heap of soil on to the base of the tree, he would puff and pant and wipe his brow and we would fly over with a handkerchief and flap his face with it. What a lovely man he was!

Pandit Nehru's visit to Broadlands was an annual affair and was usually timed to coincide with great events, such as the Commonwealth Prime Ministers Conference. What with his visits to Broadlands and ours to India we became good friends and it was my great joy to look after him each time personally.

I would call him very early with his morning cup of tea, and often find him standing on his head, his legs straight up against the wall, his arms supporting his head which was resting on a cushion. He would be wearing nothing but a loin cloth. He always spoke very gently and very quietly, and he would often greet me with: 'You ought to start the day like this, you know.' It was his belief that such a posture maintained the supply of blood to the head, eased the body, refreshed the mind and relaxed the system, and I'm sure he was right, although in my life with Mountbatten I felt as though I were permanently on my head.

At other times I would find Nehru sitting quietly in the window seat in deep meditation, or staring out at the beautiful view. As I prepared his distinctive clothes he would gaze out at the handsome portico pillars, the carefully tended lawns which run down to the River Test, and the rolling forest hills beyond, and say: 'If only the world could share this beauty and tranquillity it would be a truly heavenly place.' And I felt that I could read his thoughts, and that they were concerned with his own arid, dusty, noisy Delhi, crowded with millions of sad, proud people, for many of whom a glass of pure water was a luxury. And I felt that he would be fixing in his mind the green goodness of the grass, the wheat rippling in the fields, the clean, cool river with the gliding swans, the scent of the roses and magnolias drifting in the cool of the morning, and that it would be an everlasting memory for him of a world so far removed from his own land.

Nehru always liked to sport a fresh rose in the buttonhole of his silk frockcoat, so I would try to find a perfectly scented bud, just on the point of opening, that would see out the day. Although I never failed to provide him with a fresh one for his evening wear, he would always place the old one in a small glass of water on his dressing table. The roses at Broadlands are especially fine. They grow close by the ancient mulberry tree – which was planted by King James 1 in 1608 and still gives succulent fruit, though time has taken its toll and cement now welds its gnarled branches together – and the newer mulberry trees which our Queen planted close by it to mark her Coronation in 1953.

The week-end at Broadlands would begin with dinner on Friday which was often served late because there would frequently be late arrivals among the guests.

Visitors were expected to arrive at about six in the evening. Their guns would be taken to the gun-room, their cars to the garage, and their luggage to their rooms, so that by the time they had been welcomed and given a drink, they would be shown to their suites where all the unpacking had been completed and everything laid out neatly. The correct evening clothes would have been re-pressed if necessary and on the dressing table would be all their personal items just as if they were at home. A steaming bath would have been drawn and waiting for them, alongside a plentiful supply of hot towels. If anyone forgot to bring a bowtie, another would be put in its place, and as often as not they never noticed the substitution.

Dinner on the Friday night would be a good basic three-course meal, English fare, nothing fancy. There might be smoked salmon and roast crown or saddle of lamb. Or river salmon, a lovely ten- or twelve-pounder from the bottom of the garden. Vegetables and fruit would be home-grown with green figs, tree tomatoes and the most beautiful pears. If anybody started peeling the pears, Lord Louis would interrupt and say: 'No, no, like this.' He would then cut the pear in half, hold it upside down with the skin still on and, using a small teaspoon, scoop out the middle of the fruit as though it were a melon. It is a most efficient and practical way of eating a pear – you get all the fruit, all the juice and none of the mess.

Lord Louis was meticulous in these matters. Strawberries had to be served with their stalks on. What you then did was to make a little circle of caster sugar on your plate and fill the reservoir with thick cream fresh from the home farm. You then took a strawberry by its stalk and by twisting it enabled it to pick just the required amount of sugar and cream. If the strawberries were ever served without the stalks on in Lord Louis' presence, there would be big trouble. On very rare occasions he might opt to desnuff them individually and mash them up with the cream.

During dinner, the valets and maids would tidy up the guests' rooms and lay out the clothes for the morning, especially important if the guests were to go shooting.

An early start would be made on the Saturday morning, with a tray of tea and orange juice or whatever had been requested the night before at 7.30 a.m. This was for the gentlemen going on the shoot who would breakfast at 8.15. The ladies would have a tray breakfast in bed at about nine, just after the men had left.

An annual guest to Broadlands for the pheasant shoots was Henry Ford II, who was particularly impressed with and intrigued by the personal attention he received from us, though of course he received exactly the same attention as any other guest. Always during his stay he would beg me to return home with him and offer me the earth to do so. I had an extremely difficult time explaining to him that I was a serving Chief Petty Officer with the Royal Navy on the personal retinue of an Admiral of the Fleet and therefore not at liberty to up and go! He insisted that I was not to worry and he would 'fix' that, and indeed I am quite sure he would have set about buying me out of the Navy had I given him the least encouragement. Eventually I was to spend a short stint with him on a sabbatical from England, but by that time I had sadly left Lord Louis' employ.

Douglas Fairbanks Jnr, a lifelong friend of Lord Louis, often visited us at Broadlands, and I found him exactly the same off-screen as in *The Prisoner of Zenda, Sinbad the Sailor* and all those swashbuckling pirate films I had loved so much as a child. We would be chatting in his rooms and I would picture him leaping from the balcony, piercing the huge velvet curtains with his sword and sliding gracefully to the floor. He had kept all his impish, boyish charm and while I was laying out his beautifully tailored pinstripe suit I would be transported into yet another pirate fantasy, scarcely able to believe that I was the same urchin who had stared wide-eyed at his wonderful films.

The same hectic but minutely detailed arrangements would be made for the shoots as for everything else in Lord Louis' crowded life. Charles Smith, the butler, would set off early with the shooting lunch to one of the specially prepared keepers' cottages. Specially prepared in the sense that the walls between the front room and the kitchen had been constructed so that they could be concertinaed back to create a room large enough to seat eighteen or twenty guns. At perhaps a quarter to one I would leave the big house with the beef hotpot or whatever had been prepared for lunch. Some of the ladies might accompany me, and it was not unusual to have two queens sharing the estate car with me and the hotpot. The weather was usually cold and the afternoons short, so that lunch would be a hurried affair, but after the hotpot it was something of a tradition for a steamed pudding, syrup or apple or chocolate, to be served, and how they all wallowed in it! Few Broadlands guests refused pud!

Lord Louis would always be accompanied on the shoots by Pancho, his black labrador, specially selected by the Queen from the kennels at Sandringham. He was a most lovable creature, with one peculiarity; he was Lord Louis' dog, but if Lord Louis was away he latched on to Charles Smith. I used to take Pancho out for a quick morning stroll, as soon as I had called Lord Louis, but Pancho knew well enough who his master was. As soon as we got back, he would say goodbye to me, wagging his tail cheerfully, look at Charles, and off they would trot together. Sadly Pancho was struck down suddenly with liver cancer when Lord Louis was in New York. Despite Charles Smith's vain attempts to save him – three vets were called in – nothing could be done. In a letter Lord Louis wrote to Charles, he described Pancho as 'the greatest friend and companion I have ever known among dogs'. In time, Pancho was replaced by his son, Kelly, a glorious and lovable companion, again specially selected by the Queen.

Occasionally guests would bring their animals with them; often specifically for the shooting. The Queen's own kennel man brought Her Majesty's even-tempered labradors to the shoots in the van. The celebrated corgis rarely travelled on private home visits. Barbara Cartland always brought three pet poodles, but her visits were in the nature of flying affairs. A lifelong admirer of Lord Louis, she would call in for lunch or tea, in a mass of pink chiffon, then vanish, leaving behind her a pile of books on health and homoeopathy and a quantity of new vitamin pills and elixirs to try. Down the years she recommended to him the remarkable properties of a great variety of elixirs, herbs, vitamin capsules and royal bee jellies. One of the elixirs, a brown syrupy honey, he took quite regularly. In Barbara Cartland's view, Lord Louis was the perfect romantic figure and I'm sure she based some of her fictional heroes on him. He always seemed in very fine shape for his age, and his energy was, of course, terrific. He could exhaust many younger men, as I knew only too well!

Lord Louis did once have to have a double hernia operation, caused, I suspect, by too much horse-riding and polo, which was carried out at the Royal Naval Hospital near Portsmouth – the same hospital in which I had been isolated for my streptococcal throat. After two days there, he asked for Charles Strong, who for years had been treating him and his polo ponies with his magic 'black box of tricks'. This, his own development, used the electrical impulse Faradism system, a method of running a small electrical charge into a muscle to activate it and to disperse the congealed blood which causes the swelling and pain.

I was visiting Lord Louis at the hospital in the company of Mr Strong. Wired up around the groin, his lordship was looking pretty sore and bruised after the operation. He was going through the letters and official papers which I had brought from Broadlands as Mr Strong started his treatment. Suddenly I burst out laughing, at which Lord Louis demanded to know what was so funny. It was the sight of himself, prone on the bed, hips exposed and gyrating in an enormous hula-hoop wriggle caused by the electric waves going into his groin. Concentrating as he was, he was quite unaware of what his bottom half had been getting up to. Despite the indignity, the treatment was certainly a success and within four days Lord Louis was walking around the gardens.

Lord Louis often suffered from a rather stiff and painful neck, making it virtually impossible for him to move it left and right. Mr Strong taught me how to stretch Lord Louis' neck by cupping his head in my hands behind his ears and pulling his prone body against his own weight – all I needed was the courage to pull hard enough without feeling I was going to rip off the noble head. The results were instant – he was able to move his head quite freely after some three or four stretches.

But, to return to the shoot, almost all the men would have a go even though many of them were getting on – elderly King Gustav and Henry Ford were certainly and Sir Tommy Sopwith, the aviator, was well into his eighties, but they were a hardy bunch. Sir Tommy lived to his century, dying in 1989.

We shot home-reared pheasants, which we bred intensively in the superb woodlands. Two thousand a day would be the target, and two thousand was a pretty good bag. Occasionally some of the ladies would also shoot. The Countess of Brecknock and Lady Sopwith were regular guns with us, wearing tweed suits and smoking pipes. But how they were transformed when they appeared for dinner, radiantly feminine in their ballgowns.

King Gustav was a popular guest. He had a passion for *crêpes suzette* and would always insist on cooking them at the dining table on every visit to Broadlands, much to the apparent delight of his queen, Louise, Lord Louis' sister and the other guests. In this respect, a great boon was the introduction of the electric frying pan, as the old meths burners he had previously used had been so messy and awkward. The pancakes would be prepared for the King in the kitchen, but His Majesty would be responsible for the delicious sauce in which they were cooked. As he squeezed the fresh oranges on to the orange brandy Cointreau, the butter and sugar and hint of lemon juice, a delicious aroma would waft from him to us. As we served his *crêpes* to the assembled guests, our tongues would be hanging metaphorically, and almost literally, out.

King Gustav would have been in his eighties at that time, Queen Louise in her seventies. She too had her little ways. She told us that she always carried a card in her handbag stating: 'I am the Queen of Sweden.' We wondered why.

'Well,' she explained, 'I roam around London alone, and I often nip across the road from my hotel to Harrods. Just imagine how inconvenient it would be if I got run over and nobody knew who I was.'

I was particularly fond of the Swedish Royal Family, who, in true Mountbatten fashion, were extremely practical. They were a close family, of course. Shortly after she became Queen of Sweden, Louise was standing on the steps of St Paul's at the conclusion of some imposing state occasion and one of the family said to Queen Louise as a huge Rolls drew up: 'This is your car, Your Majesty.'

To which she replied: 'Oh no, that couldn't possibly be for me, it must be for some queen or other.' She really could not grasp in the early days of her marriage that she was indeed a queen.

Two or three times a year we would visit them in Sweden, staying at Ulriksdal, a very romantic palace set deep in the forest. When we arrived, the Queen would show Lord Louis to his suite and then grab me by the arm and say: 'You come with me, Evans.' Then she would wave at the accompanying ADCs, shoo them off, saying: 'You are all down there somewhere,' and take me down the passage to my room which had, of course, to be close by Mountbatten's. 'I've put my own little radio in there,' she would add. 'It's a bit temperamental but I know how much you like the radio.' She would have picked out a few books for me and left them in my room. 'You simply must read these,' she would say. 'I have chosen them myself.' She always made herself responsible for the flowers in my room, and there would always be a bowl of fresh fruit specially selected by the sweet-natured woman. She made just as much fuss of me as she did of Lord Louis – perhaps more, I think.

On these visits, Their Majesties would take us to the sixteenth-century Court Theatre at Drottningholm, beautifully preserved with all the old trappings and the antique revolving sets. King Gustav would show us round and suddenly grab me by the arm to point out something special, whereupon Lord Louis would say: 'What about me? What about me?'

To which the King would reply: 'Oh, you've done all this, Dickie. Evans hasn't seen this one before.'

The King was also a great geologist and archaeologist and had a wonderful collection of fossils and semi-precious stones, which he was so proud to escort us round. On one visit he took us, wrapped in waterproofs, to see the *Wasa*, a recently exhumed Swedish warship which had lain preserved in the river mud for over 350 years. Now she had been raised, together with many relics, sailors' hats, shoes, breeches, coins, combs, cannons, and carvings of lions and mythical beasts. Like our own *Mary Rose* at Portsmouth she was kept in a permanent fine haze of water-spray so that she should not disintegrate.

But back to Broadlands.

My most vivid memory of a Broadlands shoot was one day when I found myself helping the Queen off with her wellington boots as Her Majesty arrived at the lunch.

Her Majesty was in the head keeper's cottage. Whereas everyone else had to take their boots off in the yard where there was a bucket and brush with which to scrub off the worst of the dirt, the Queen came directly indoors to take hers off in the fireplace. I had arrived with the hotpot as usual and we were making final preparations when Lord Louis said: 'Evans, help Her Majesty off with her boots.'

I knelt down as if to be knighted and grabbed hold of the boot as Her Majesty offered it to me. It was maroony-brown and close-fitting. She was balancing with one hand on the mantelpiece, and I kept tugging gently, trying to get the damn muddy, slippery thing off without tipping Her Majesty over.

Next thing I knew a hand had been placed on the top of my head as she sought to keep her balance. 'Haven't you got a lovely curly head of hair?' she said.

I always felt strangely honoured about that occasion. It was a glorious moment in my life, and it has stayed in the back of my mind ever since.

After lunch, the ladies would join the shoot which continued until the light began to fade, when the whole party would troop back into the house, freezing cold. We had huge log fires ready for them, with crumpets and marshmallows and chestnuts roasting by the fire. While they warmed themselves they would toast their own crumpets. There would also be fresh honey from the farm and homemade jam, blackcurrant or redcurrant, from the garden. As well as all this, there would be a variety of sandwiches and homemade cakes, a glorious traditional country-house tea, with hot chocolate or Bovril for those who preferred them.

Then there would be a necessary lull, a jigsaw puzzle, a book, or maybe a tour round part of the house. Time for a zizz. A bath and a zizz. Or possibly games for the more alert. Then they would dress for dinner.

Saturday night dinner tended to be early and more rushed than the Friday night version, because after dinner there would be the cinema. Most of the guests were great cinema buffs. In the later years, Lord Mountbatten's connections in the film world led to the gift from Sam Spiegel and Mike Frankovitch, the Hollywood moguls, of two modern 35mm projectors, so that the films could be shown all the way through as their makers had intended. The projectors came with a screen, curtains, dimmer lights, a projection box, the works, and everything was set up in a lovely old oak-panelled room upstairs. A small stage was constructed on which were placed the cosy armchairs for the VIPs, while we sat in front of, and below them. Before this we had had to do the best we could with a little whirly-bird 16mm contraption buzzing away at the back of the room and all the tiresome rigmarole of laying the speakers and the wires in one of the big drawing-rooms, not to mention the long intervals while they rewound the film between reels. 35mm projection also enabled us to enjoy a much wider selection of films, including the most up-to-date.

The staff would always be the last into the cinema, and we would find the Queen or the most important of the guests sitting in armchairs in the middle of the room waiting for us to finish clearing the dinner table. Lord Louis would quickly become impatient and bawl down the stairs: 'Come on, come on!' but he would never start the film until we had all assembled. Invariably worn out as the staff would be in the middle of an exhausting week-end, there was no escaping to bed, and if I did sneak off he became quite narked. He loved films and expected us all to enjoy them too.

Most of the films *were* wonderful. Lord Louis was one of only three people in the world – the others being Winston Churchill and the Queen Mother – to have been accorded a special privilege by the Hollywood Motion Picture Academy.

This entitled him to ask for any film of his choice and it would be sent to him. We often had previews and one felt very privileged to be watching films like *Mary Poppins* and *Those Magnificent Men in Their Flying Machines* before their release to the rest of the world. Prince Charles, then about nine or ten, joined us for *Those Magnificent Men* and both he and I creased up in laughter. The Prince has the greatest sense of humour and we could neither of us control ourselves as we watched the German officer trying to fly his machine by the instruction book and inevitably crash-landing in a cess pit. (I was always laughing when I was with the assembled Royal Family. They are the happiest, most humorous family you could ever hope to meet. Your sides ached with laughter whenever they were together.) Before the main feature we would watch a cartoon to give us the atmosphere of a real cinema, but sadly we never got round to iced lollies. Which reminds me . . .

One very hot summer's day Lord Louis and I were travelling down in the Jaguar to Uckfield to stay with Lord Rupert Neville. Lord Louis asked if we had anything in the car to drink.

'No,' I said, 'but we could stop and get a lolly.'

'Get a what?'

'An iced lolly.'

'What on earth is that?'

'Well, it's a sort of frozen drink on a stick.'

'Good, good, let's get one of those. Where do we find them?'

We drove on until we came to a small village shop, and there were these two old dears nattering in the corner and we in our shirtsleeves. I directed him to the freezer and we went rooting all through it before coming upon the cornets.

'Are these them? What about this one?' He was holding up a choc ice.

'No, no, we just want the plain orange stick things,' I said. 'Not the ones with the ice-cream middles.'

By the time we had found them I was aware of a whirl of excitement behind us.

I turned round and one of the old biddies was staring covertly at us and muttering to her friend: 'Oh, it's him, it's him. It is.'

Her friend was saying: 'No, really, I don't think so. It couldn't be, and he wouldn't be buying lollies, would he?'

'What are they saying?' Lord Louis whispered to me.

I said: 'I think they are talking about us.'

As I was paying for the lollies, I said I would treat him, since he was providing the car. He left the shop while I was doing what was necessary and I heard the first biddy say: 'I'm sure it *was* that Lord Mountbatten.'

'It did look like him,' said her friend, 'but no, it couldn't possibly be. Could it?'

This was the first time Lord Louis had ever tasted such a thing as a lolly, and like a child he always loved them thereafter so that, whenever we were travelling on a particularly hot day, he would throw a little glance in my direction and lick his lips and I would stop and buy us lollies. It became a regular occurrence.

Talking of Uckfield, I remember one time when, staying the night with Lord Rupert Neville at Uckfield House, I had asked the cook to provide scrambled eggs and bacon for Lord Louis' breakfast. Sadly, in the morning, Cookie was indisposed and the housemaid had to prepare the food. She admitted that she couldn't even boil the proverbial egg and was terrified at having to cook his lordship's breakfast, so I said, 'Don't worry. Melt a little butter in a pan, put in two eggs and shuffle them about with a fork.' She produced a marvellous egg – neither scrambled nor an omelette – which Lord Louis enjoyed enormously. After that, he would always ask his hostess for 'Uckfield Egg', never giving a thought that ambassadors' wives from the Argentine or Fiji had no idea what he was talking about and had probably never heard of Uckfield!

With his distinctive bearing and handsome face Lord Louis was frequently recognised, and I could understand why. In the train on the way to Sandringham one shooting winter week-end, I was stretching my legs in the corridor outside the compartment reserved for Lord Louis, who was busy as usual with his despatch boxes. A lad of about fourteen and his mother came past. The boy snatched a look at Lord Louis and shouted to his mother: 'Lord Mountbatten is in that carriage, Mum!'

At which she promptly boxed his ears, saying: 'Lord Mountbatten wouldn't be travelling on this train.'

I felt for that poor lad and his stinging ears. She was so convinced that she never even looked to find out.

Lord Louis' eating habits were sometimes most peculiar. We always travelled with a picnic basket and one of his greatest joys, while on the road, was sardines eaten straight from the tin with chunky bread and toasted Bovril sandwiches. I might be driving him down to Wales, while he was working on a speech, and he would suddenly grab a sardine out of a tin, wop it into a slice of French bread and continue to discuss the speech he was working while spluttering sardine at me and filling my earhole with sandwich. He had another penchant for iced chocolate milkshakes, or, in cold weather, a hot Bovril or a hot chocolate.

Mountbatten drank only in moderation, preferring cider and beer to spirits. Most of the time he drank homemade lemon drink made by Charles the butler, bottles of which I had to produce to order wherever we went. He had also invented his own pick-me-up which was a raw egg thrown into an orange brandy and shaken with crushed ice. To me it looked absolutely revolting and I couldn't touch it, but he swore by it, and often asked for one, especially after riding and when he felt tired.

He succeeded in giving up smoking whilst I was working for him, for which I was profoundly grateful, especially during our long car trips. Sometimes, though, he would puff a cigar after special dinners.

On those not too infrequent occasions when we had film people staying at Broadlands, we would do without a film on the Saturday night. It was considered that since their lives were all films, they would be better entertained by *not* having to watch one. Instead they might all go out to dinner with special friends.

Sundays would often begin with horse-riding, followed by morning service at Romsey Abbey. Lord Louis was as methodical about his riding as about everything else. As a young man he had been a keen polo player; now when time allowed he would take a two-, three-, or four-hour ride across the beautiful Hampshire countryside. He had all the routes measured and timed and he always carried secateurs with him so he could cut back overhanging branches from the 'rides'. I had to make sure that he had a stiff white card and a clip pencil in the breast pocket of his riding jacket, on which he would scribble a list of necessary improvements to gates, fences, hedges and river-banks. He would also sometimes prepare his major speeches while out riding and jot down endless memos.

If guests did not care to ride, Lord Louis persuaded them to try something else. If they expressed an interest in fishing, the bailiffs would accompany them, providing rods and everything necessary. I remember one occasion when it was time for church, but little Princess Anne was nowhere to be found. As I expected, she was in the stables. There she was, hair all over the place, with our head groom, Arthur Birch, just about to scoop up another load of horse dung and straw with her bare hands. As soon as I mentioned church, she said: 'Oh bother,' and rushed off to the house, where she dashed upstairs to Nanny. Within a minute or two this demure little princess came trotting down the stairs, all in pink, a little beret on her head. But the last Amen had scarcely left the congregation's lips before she was back and changed and down to the stables where she would be washing and sponging down the sweating beasts before lunch.

Sunday lunch was, of course, traditional good solid fare. Roast beef and bread and butter pudding, that sort of thing. There was an unspoken understanding that guests would leave soon after lunch. The Queen left at tea-time; occasionally some stragglers would stay on as long as possible, finding Broadlands such a joy.

Although, despite the extra work involved, I certainly enjoyed these week-ends, it was not uncommon for us to be leaving for a world tour down one drive as the week-end guests were leaving down the other, and on these occasions I was under special pressure. It was a hard task to fit in the tour packing while working hard at Broadlands caring for our famous guests after a hectic week in London. Frequently we would fly off at four in the morning and find ourselves in North Africa for breakfast with all the C-in-Cs before travelling on to our main stop-over that same evening. From Broadlands to the tropical desert heat of Africa in just a few hours.

*   *   *

It was inevitable that I would have my favourites amongst all the guests at Broadlands, although it was a matter of pride to me that I should treat all guests exactly the same. Among them were Montgomery of Alamein and Field Marshal Bill Slim, whom Lord Louis regarded as the greatest soldier England had ever produced. The nicest man of all perhaps was Prince Rainier. He came to stay with his beautiful wife not long after they were married. I had fallen in love with Grace Kelly many years before (who hadn't?) but in my case the passion was of a very particular nature because Brenda, the love of my young life, was so very much like Grace Kelly with her clear blue eyes, her fair hair and perfect complexion.

Other frequent guests included Her Royal Highness, Princess Alice of Greece, who was Lord Louis' sister, Prince Philip's mother. She always wore the plain grey habit of the nun's order which she had formed, so we had to be especially tactful at Broadlands when it came to serving her in her suite. We would knock loudly, then wait patiently for about five minutes until we heard a stern 'Come in!' The reason for this was readily apparent because the room would be clouded with smoke. She preferred that her cigarette-smoking and her love of detective fiction should not be public knowledge; but she would sit most serenely while we went about our business with just a glint of mischief in her eye as if to say, 'You won't say a word about catching me smoking, will you?'

Conversation was never dull when Princess Alice and her sister, the Queen of Sweden, were together. The years had impaired their hearing, and much shouting added to the hilarity. They were great and very sweet ladies, very much Mountbattens, and the world is the poorer for their passing.

Most of the royal families who visited us at Broadlands were Lord Louis' relatives, as a result of Queen Victoria marrying off her children to all the European princes and princesses. The young Lord Louis had once been hopelessly in love with Marie, the daughter of the Czar of Russia, after visiting her family at the Kremlin. She was murdered, of course, during the Revolution, along with her parents, brother and sisters, their retainers and the family pets. All the remaining royal houses of Europe are linked by blood to the House of

Windsor, and I have found every member, without exception, to be charming and intelligent. But I am sometimes a little startled when I see that young boys and girls I taught to fish off the Donegal coast have now become kings and queens and have princes and princesses of their own. How quickly life passes us by!

A regular visitor and another favourite of mine was Shirley Maclaine. She and Lord Louis had become acquainted at a Hollywood party when a game was played in the course of which guests were paired off and lashed together. They had to extricate themselves as best they could. Lord Louis had been lucky enough to have been paired with Shirley Maclaine. (The secretary was also fortunate, finding himself tied to the curvaceous Claudia Cardinale.) Shirley is an extremely intelligent woman and a very bright cookie who spent several weekends at Broadlands over the years.

Sir Malcolm Sargent, the great conductor, was another visitor. He was always impeccably turned out and had quite a reputation as a ladies' man. Indeed, he was rather more Lady Louis' friend. He was a bundle of fun and a great practical joker, and the house was always full of joviality when he stayed. In the evenings, he was always prepared to give us a turn on the piano. Although I did not know it at the time, he was very ill with cancer, and died not long after we had welcomed him at Broadlands. I always wished I had had the time to get to know him better.

Noël Coward visited Broadlands frequently. He had known Lord and Lady Louis for many years, and had given them the first public performance of 'Mad Dogs and Englishmen', when he was staying with them at the Casa Medina in Malta. He also used Lord Louis' war-time adventures on board H M S *Kelly* as the basis of his film *In Which We Serve*. Lord Louis returned the compliment years later when he fought for Noël Coward to be given a knighthood. Towards the end of his life, Sir Noël became rather forgetful, as did several of Lord Louis' contemporaries.

King Bhumibol and Queen Sirikit of Thailand came to stay but they brought their own entourage and I have to say I was extremely grateful for that. Far and away the most difficult guest we ever had was Princess Pahlav, the sister of the Shah of Persia. She arrived very late, seriously holding up the serving of dinner, then opened her voluminous trunks and slung everything on to the floor, ordering the poor old housekeeper at eleven o'clock at night to have everything clean, pressed and ready by the morning.

The Duke and Duchess of Windsor visited us on their only trip to Britain since their exile. It was a traumatic time for all of us. They had travelled over on the SS *United States* – a great liner at that time and holder of the Blue Riband for the quickest Atlantic crossing – and Lord Louis and I went on board at Southampton to meet them. (Incidentally, Lord Louis and I had ourselves taken passage on the same liner, with the same cabins, only a month or two before on our return from the States.) Their own valet and maid had been dropped off at Le Havre to return to their Paris home with the luggage from their American trip, so it fell to me to look after the Duke at Broadlands. Without his man, the Duke was quite at odds, his cabin disorganised, so I went straight into action and completed the packing. He remained responsible for his collection of pipes and a lovely old leather medical case which was full of arsenical crystals, various forms of strychnine and a great variety of peculiar herbs and homoeopathic remedies which the Royal Family always carried about with them. I was told that the Duke and Duchess would only have their 'night luggage' with them, but their night luggage turned out to be fourteen huge cases of the traditional leather variety, exceptionally weighty. The Duchess was in the next-door cabin with a lady steward helping her, because she too was without staff. As I chatted to the Duke, it was impossible to be unaware of the aura of sadness which surrounded him.

The purpose of their visit was to unveil a memorial to Queen Mary, the Duke's mother, and the ceremony was to be on the Monday, so it had been arranged that they should spend the week-end at Broadlands, which is just eight miles from Southampton, and that we should keep the whole thing very quiet.

The first thing the Duke said to me on being introduced was: 'Shall I call you Taffy?'

Since he was typical ex-Navy, it followed naturally that

every Evans would be a Taffy, although I absolutely hated the nickname.

'I'd rather you didn't, sir,' I said.

'Very well, we'll stick to Chief Petty Officer, shall we?'

'Yes, please,' I said, 'I should like that.'

Then he went on to ask whether was I from Wales. He did so like to speak the Welsh language, he said. He started nattering away and I had to tell him that I was very sorry, but I could not even give him a good morning or a good evening in Welsh. I added that I had come from a northern steel worker's family. It was only later that I was to discover that my grandfather hailed from the Rhondda. As we continued packing he inquired further about my origins, and I explained about my evacuation and my upbringing in the Yorkshire wolds. He seemed so very interested and continued to probe into my childhood, my memories of the war, my naval career.

Our two very distinctive cars – light blue with black tops – were waiting, including a small Jaguar on the bonnet of which stood the silver model of a sailor with semaphore flags presented to Lord Louis by the Duke, then Prince of Wales, on the occasion of his being best man at the Mountbatten wedding in 1922. Also on the roof was the red and gold crown shield of the Royal Family. There were a few dockies standing around, and I heard several cries of 'Good old Teddy!' The Duke was greatly moved; we all were.

The royal party climbed into the Jaguar, and I followed with the luggage – most of it! – and a policeman in the big Zodiac estate wagon bearing on its bonnet a replica of the silver sailor. With a discreet police escort we slowly left the docks.

On the road to Broadlands there were clusters of people, most of them elderly, who had come out to see us pass. They had their handkerchiefs out and many of them were weeping openly. I cried too. Here was a king, after some thirty years in exile, returning for the first time since the war and possibly for the very last time, to the country which had rejected him over the woman he so desperately loved and who was with him now by his side half a century later, on his way to pay final tribute to his mother, Queen Mary. He was adored, and I adored him. My heart went out to him for I could imagine what a traumatic experience it must have been.

We continued our conversation throughout the week-end, which was a deliberately low-key affair. The only other visitor was Lord Louis' daughter, Lady Patricia. The Duke and the Duchess had walks in the garden, planted a tree, spent quiet evenings, quiet meals and enjoyed early nights. It was a fine week-end; the weather could not have been kinder. They were given time to regain their strength and prepare themselves for the ordeal ahead, because, of course, it was a great strain for them. The Duke was an old man by then with chronic eye trouble, which meant that he wore dark glasses most of the time, and had to take great care when walking.

When he left us to prepare for the unveiling in London, my duty was done and it was goodbye. I felt once more that I had been especially honoured and privileged to have been close to a man whose personal destiny had shaped that of our nation. Even during those few days I had experienced his passionate understanding and his gentle and kindly nature. The next time he came home to England was in his coffin, and he came home to be buried at Windsor. No one was sadder than I at his passing, and I shall always treasure the memory of the short time I spent with him.

We had a great many honeymooners at Broadlands. When Princess Elizabeth, now the Queen, married Prince Philip, they honeymooned there. So did the present Prince and Princess of Wales.

I had the pleasant responsibility of looking after young Prince Juan Carlos, now King of Spain, and his young bride from Greece. I had no idea that one day he would be King of Spain, but Lord Louis assured me that he would. We had visits from Princess Alexandra from time to time, the Duke of Kent, Prince Michael, but it required no significant alteration in our routine; they were just part of the family.

Prince Charles was at boarding school, unable to spend much time at Broadlands, but he paid us occasional visits with his parents. In 1965, I cashed in all my bonus/gratuity I had received on leaving the Navy, put it together with my modest savings and blew the whole £749 on my own little Triumph Spitfire sports car. I also installed a Grundig record player, because this was in the days before cassette players had been invented. Anyway, I was proudly cleaning the car outside my flat one day when Prince Charles, then a sixteen-year-old, came out and asked whether the car was mine. I told him it was, and, having crawled all over the car, he became interested in the Grundig. I explained how it worked and pushed in the small single record it played, which it flung out when finished.

'We haven't got one of those in any of our cars,' he said.

'Ah well,' I said, 'it's quite a new thing.'

I often wonder if Prince Charles's love of sports cars in general and little blue ones in particular may be traced back to that occasion.

It was at Sandringham, not Broadlands, that I became more closely acquainted with Prince Andrew and Prince Edward. One day I dashed, as usual, out of Lord Louis' suite straight into an Unidentified Flying Object, which on closer inspection turned out to be a plastic skittle hurled by a very young Prince Andrew at his father along the corridor. Prince Philip had been hiding in the deep doorways and popping his head out from time to time. You took your life into your hands when the young royals were at play. Edward was altogether quieter and shyer than Andrew and used to cling tightly to Prince Charles's leg. He seemed so fond of his eldest brother.

After a while I became so experienced at the Broadlands week-ends that there was no longer any need for me to be briefed by Charles the butler; indeed I was so expert that guests would ask me endlessly for advice on all manner of things. How to behave in the presence of royalty was something which made some of our less regular visitors nervous. But while I was always on hand with excellent advice for the guests, there were occasions when my own behaviour left something to be desired.

One day in Lord Louis' room, when things had got a bit on top of me, the telephone rang when I was growing frantic and least wanted it to. I picked up the receiver and shouted 'Yes?' into the mouthpiece. This was quite uncharacteristic because one never knew who might be at the other end of the line. I heard in response a little chuckle and I knew immediately that it was Prince Philip. He quite understood and said: 'Is he giving you a hard time, Evans?'

But it must not be thought that all our guests at Broadlands were royals or celebrities. Each year a small invalid car would arrive (usually in the lull between the social and the shooting seasons) and a legless old gentleman in his seventies would roll out. As a boy seaman of seventeen he had been befriended by Lord Louis' parents after he lost his legs in action. Lord Louis had continued the friendship. I looked after this old chap and ensured that he received exactly the same treatment as all the other guests. He and his host always had a great time reminiscing about the old days at sea.

Throughout Broadlands those grand old days were visibly remembered. Coats of arms, plaques, ceremonial trumpets and ensigns commemorated military and naval history in a dignified and heart-stirring way. In the Ship's Passage, presented to him by Lady Louis, were models of all the ships on which Lord Louis had served, with a painted background representing the harbour or port with which it was associated. At the end of the corridor was a model of HMS *President*, a small, black, wooden-hulled ship moored alongside the Embankment. That is the official ship of all the men who are attached to the Admiralty in London, and it takes pride of place as Mountbatten's last ship; it was also mine.

But perhaps the most priceless treasure of all was the white ensign which had been flying on the ill-fated HMS *Kelly*, under Mountbatten's command, when she was torpedoed off Crete in 1941, and finally sunk. This relic was presented to Lord Louis at the twenty-fifth anniversary of the *Kelly* reunion by one of the sailors who brought it out from under his jacket. It was ripped and torn, shattered with shell-holes and filthy dirty, never having been washed or mended, but it was mounted ready to be placed in a glass case above the model of the *Kelly*.

While we were mounting it, our dear housekeeper intervened and said: 'Oh, we'll have to wash it. It's filthy.'

'No, no,' I replied. 'You can't possibly do that. Have you no sense of history?'

But since she was adamant that it must be washed, I said: 'Well, we'll ask himself.'

When we did, we were rewarded with the same fusillade that I had received when I had suggested repairing the dent in his ceremonial sword. So the ensign hangs mounted on the wall, filthy and in need of a good mending, as any self-respecting housekeeper would say.

Incidentally, when the old sailor presented Lord Louis with the ensign at the reunion, Lord Louis riposted: 'I've a good mind to put you on a charge for stealing Her Majesty's property, but in the circumstances we'll overlook this matter.' And let him off, with a caution.

As the *Kelly* was sinking off Crete, Lord Louis, who was the last to leave the bridge, flung himself into the oil-covered sea. It was then he admits to having done the stupidest thing in his life. On entering the sea, he threw off his steel helmet which he had been wearing at action stations on the bridge, shortly after which the German planes swooped down and machine-gunned the *Kelly* survivors in the sea. He had never felt so naked in his life and deeply regretted having cast away his tin hat!

On arrival in Alexandria he was met by a grinning Prince Philip, who said: 'You look like a Kentucky minstrel!'

The oil had blackened the survivors' faces and just the whites of their eyes shone through.

Lord Louis was obsessively interested in his own family history. He compiled a complete family lineage and relationship table and built up a collection of family portraits dating back to Charlemagne. These were each identified and numbered, with a catalogue of family portraits as complete as anything in the land. As for the film and photograph archives, these proved invaluable when it came to making the twelve-part television series about Lord Louis' career, *The Life and Times of Lord Mountbatten*. They included visual records of almost every visit and function, every tree-planting, every week-end and every tour. Uniquely valuable too were the official tour diaries, which covered each tour from beginning to end.

There is one subject which excites prurient interest whenever the Royal Family is mentioned. Contrary to endless newspaper articles and ill-informed gossip about the lack of closeness amongst the Royal Family and their supposed marital difficulties, I can but state how I found the situation during our numerous visits to them or their happy times at Broadlands.

Never once, either during the state occasions or more intimately during the private visits, did I observe anything other than a pleasant, harmonious and often extremely humorous atmosphere. I have seen as the Queen was chased up the great stone staircases by Prince Philip, as she squealed and giggled with delight – so natural and so loving. And I have observed the happy family hour between tea and supper when the children's playtime became dangerous to life and limb. Even on state occasions, when Her Majesty was dressed in a long white dress and dazzling diamond tiara with the blue Garter Riband, it was not unusual to see her, just before setting off for some ceremony or procession in a lobby, putting down on the floor dinner for the numerous small dogs which required to be fed. Or the beloved Queen Mother, already wearing her magnificent Garter Robes, having to be coaxed away from the television while she desperately clung on to see her horse running in a race, reluctantly leaving the television and muttering: 'What one must sacrifice for one's country!'

Criticism is often made too of the Queen's dress sense, her headscarf and wellingtons and tweed skirt. She likes nothing better than to tramp the muddy fields with her dogs, so what could be more practical than her favourite costume? Do people really expect their queen to go out on a wet and windy November day, in the ice or in the snow, wearing a velvet robe and tiara? When she attends country affairs in a private capacity, she dresses appropriately – the only practical thing to do.

Many people further criticise the Royal Family's love of field sports, in particular the pheasant shoots. Pheasants are not, of course, wild birds threatened by extinction. So many more are bred than shot during the season that this is one species of game bird whose existence is not threatened. By shooting reared pheasants during the limited season under strictly controlled rules – for instance, shooting cock-birds only, leaving hens free to produce their eggs – the continuity of the species is ensured. Nor is it an easy matter to shoot at and hit a fast-flying pheasant. I have seen many more escape than get shot, especially during the second half of the day when the gentlemen have had a good lunch and perhaps a sloe-gin or two. On the Broadlands estate the standard of shooting *always* deteriorated during the afternoon!

Landowners go to great expense and give employment to hundreds of people on their private estates, rearing game for the country's tables, in much the same way as poultry farmers rear chickens. The main difference, of course, is that game pheasants have at least a sporting chance of escaping an untimely end, which is more than the poor battery chickens get at the end of the electrified knife and conveyor-belt system.

I feel much the same about fox-hunting. The few members of the Royal Family who go out with the hunt perhaps once or twice during the season do so for the pleasure of the riding and the exercise. They never participate in any way in the killing of a fox. Indeed it is very rare for a Reynard to be caught – he is dead cunning and outwits the hunt far more often than not.

Broadlands was, then, a favourite retreat for virtually all the royals, including the Queen, who came at least once a year, usually around the time of her wedding anniversary, but also for special occasions such as weddings and christenings. Above all, though, these house parties were great fun, even for us staff who had to put in so much hard work. However, this palled into insignificance when we thought of the wonderful company and the privilege we had of sharing the private moments of the world's greatest figures.

Chapter Six:
On the Move Again

In preparation for this book I made a list of the countries I visited on my tours with Lord Louis. After I got to fifty I gave up. I know that between 1960 and 1969 I stayed at three royal palaces in Sweden (Ulriksdal, Drottningholm and Sophiero). I was the guest of King Olav at Skaugum in the Norwegian mountains, and the King and Queen of Denmark at Fredensborg. At Wolfsgarten in Frankfurt we stayed with Prince Louis of Hesse, who would have been the reigning monarch if Mr Hitler had not messed about with Europe's royalty; with King Baudouin and Queen Fabiola at the Royal Palace in Brussels; with the King of Siam in Bangkok. Naturally I became familiar with all our own royal houses.

We paid a regular annual visit to Balmoral, nearly always arriving at three in the morning because Lord Louis would have taken the salute at the Edinburgh Castle Tattoo on the way up. It was all very well for him, because, having changed in a layby out of Naval Ball Dress into old corduroys, he could lie flat out in the back of the Daimler, but I had to sit in a small front box seat, nodding off all the way to Balmoral. Then up again early next morning to start the day's shooting on the grouse moors.

Personally I preferred Windsor. To my way of thinking, there is not another place in the world that can give you the same sense of history as Windsor Castle. It is steeped in centuries of tradition and, despite the clever modernisations, you still sometimes feel that you are walking with Henry VIII. However, the castle is on a direct flight path out of Heathrow and huge jumbo jets whistle past the windows. There is a story of an American tourist who was visiting Windsor Castle and was heard to say: 'Gee, what a beautiful place, but why did they have to build it here right next to the airport?'

Windsor was not built with bathrooms, so these had to be cunningly designed into the corridors by closing the passage doors at each end and opening the panels to reveal the bath.

At Windsor the Royal Household Stewards Room is a large senior staff dining-hall with a long refectory table where one is waited on by young staff hoping to be selected as footmen. One's hierarchical position is clearly evident by one's place at the table. When our visits were private ones with few other members of the family in residence, I would usually find myself at the head of the table, next to the Duke of Edinburgh's staff. But during Garter Weekend at Windsor Castle, when most of the family came to stay, I would gradually be moved some eight places further down the table as the week-end progressed and more and more royal visitors arrived for the Ascot house party which followed the Garter Ceremony. Lord Louis rarely stayed for Ascot, and we would normally leave after lunch on Sunday. He was not fond of horse races, yet he loved polo and riding was his greatest passion.

This sense of hierarchy was very jealously preserved as much among the Royal Household as among the royals themselves. We all remained most respectful towards the senior members of the Household, notably the Queen Mother's staff, most of whom had been in service for many years and were shown the courtesy and attention that befitted their seniority.

I stayed at the presidential palaces in Delhi, Bombay, Ethiopia, Rawalpindi, Sierra Leone, Kandy, Sarawak, Kuala Lumpur, Malaya and Monrovia, where they no longer talk of palaces, so officially it was an executive mansion. At twenty governor-general's houses. At seventeen British embassies. At numerous military bases, including SHAPE in Paris, Fort Bragg and Fort Worth, Pearl Harbor, and dozens of others. At Fort Bragg the paratroopers made me an honorary dough-boy, at Forth Worth an honorary ranger, but Lady Mountbatten became a Kentucky colonel at the same ceremony, so she outranked us all. I have stayed at most of the finest hotels in the world, from the Waldorf-Astoria in New York to tropical paradises in the South Seas. We stayed with film magnates, great industrialists, kings, emperors.

I flew in Doves and Herons, Boeings and Andovers, VC10s and DC8s, Caravelles and Constellations, Tridents and Dakotas; in New Zealand Sunderland flying boats and in Grumnan Goose amphibians, in the private jet belonging to the President of Nigeria, in planes of the Queen's Flight, in military aircraft from here, there and everywhere, and in probably every type of helicopter and hovercraft in service.

Together with Mountbatten I travelled from the Aztec pyramids in Mexico to the site of the original Olympic Games in Delphi, from the Taj Mahal to the Kariba Dam, from Acapulco to Zanzibar. I was always within calling distance of Lord Louis, whether we were in an aircraft being tossed about over the Rangoon Range of mountains of Burma or in muddy trenches with the troops in Borneo. I scarcely ever spent two successive nights in the same bed. I accompanied him on twenty-four principal tours.

Often I thought to myself that my job was the most demanding ever devised, but in my heart I knew that it was also the most rewarding, thrilling and adventurous life anyone could have dreamed of. I doubt whether there is a man alive today who could better it.

My first world tour was in 1961. We set off in October and flew straight in our converted RAF Comet to El Adem, the transit post where all military flights to the Far East stopped to refuel. It was very, very hot and we spent the night in a tin hut. In the middle of the night, one of our principal staff officers, a senior admiral, was awakened in his cubicle which adjoined mine to find his suit rising into the air and being tugged through a grating on the end of a fishing line. Although the rooms had been passed as entirely secure, there was a small but necessary air vent in the ceiling, which had proved irresistible to enterprising young Arabs.

From El Adem, we travelled to the Maldives, a tiny group of islands so flat that you would have thought the slightest rough sea would have washed them away. As we travelled we picked up the area commanders-in-chief, and since there was no time for meetings on the ground, they would all take passage with us. High-level discussions, you might say, at 39,000 feet!

After Kuala Lumpur, where Lord Louis had to acquaint himself with the latest news of the ongoing Malayan war, we flew to Singapore for discussions with the Prime Minister, Lee Kuan Yew, who had been a student standing on the steps of the City Hall when Lord Louis received the surrender of the Japanese and had been one of his greatest admirers ever since. Then on to Bangkok.

We only had twenty-four hours in the Thai capital, where we were accommodated as guests of the King and Queen in Postanaluk in our own little palace within the grounds of the royal palace. Fortunately, our short stay was long enough to take in a trip to the original royal palace, reminiscent of *The King and I*, and to make an early morning visit to the floating market.

There was also a state banquet in the gardens. Thailand is one of the places where the monarch is revered as a god, so it did not take me long to realise why the King and Queen were always on carpets, and why everyone who approached within four feet of the monarch had to go down on their knees. This edict applied equally to the Royal Family, the Princes, the Lord Chamberlain, everyone.

Naturally, I had an automatic fellow feeling for those serving the food, and my heart went out to them when I observed the difficulties under which they laboured. For they had to present these vast dishes of food aloft, heads bowed under the dishes, while remaining on their knees. I was astounded too by their costumes. What lovely breeches, I thought at first, but they were not breeches, they were blue velvet pantaloons, slit at the back, so that when they turned round you caught flashes of bare thigh. Conventional breeches could never have stood up to all that kneeling and would have ripped open.

It was an extraordinary set-up. I had five boys to look after me, and I could not even open a door for myself without one or other of these lads dashing forward and getting there first. Our bedrooms in this palace had mirror glass in the ceilings, stained-glass windows and swing doors like those in saloon bars in my beloved western films. None the less, they were extremely luxurious and the marble floors were shiny enough to see your face in. Naturally, everything was air-conditioned.

For the state banquet the garden of the palace was alight with a myriad of coloured lanterns and the food was a remarkable mixture of all sorts of exotic ingredients. There were octopi and little pink things that looked like worms; there were shaved coconuts served in bowls of ice with the most unforgettable fresh coconut ice-cream inside them.

In the years that were to follow I became as expert as Lord Louis at dealing with the odd dishes that we were sometimes expected to eat. We would glance at each other when some revolting stuff was placed before us. Then, knowing that in this case it was quite impossible, we would say: 'Oh, we just couldn't eat another thing – we're absolutely full.' No matter that we might be absolutely starving, we would beg forgiveness and explain that we had had such an enormous meal at our last port of call, or that we had a touch of gippy tummy. We would tell all sorts of exaggerated lies, but I must admit that we would do it very charmingly. It was not unknown for us to return to our sleeping quarters absolutely starving and ready to give our left ear – or whatever the going rate was – for a banana.

We never took a chef with us on the tours, and by and large we loved 'going native'. In most places, the traditional dishes were very, very good. Even in the poorest countries, we would usually get adequate breakfasts. In India, where the habits of the British Raj lingered, we were always given eggs and bacon.

A dance floor had been laid in the garden of the Bangkok royal palace and the King got up to play the trumpet with the jazz group which had been assembled for the occasion. Queen Sirikit just sat there and watched. She has been acknowledged to be one of the most beautiful women in the world, but her English was limited.

Later Lord Louis was to describe to me what followed: 'Do you know what she asked me? She kept asking would I open a flower with her.' Lord Louis had sat there sweltering in the heat and wondering what on earth she could mean, but she continued to look at him expectantly and pose this most mystifying of questions. 'What was I supposed to do? Would a dish of flowers arrive and would I have to partake in some exotic ceremony or other? All the time she kept looking at me as if to say: Well, are we going to open a flower? Naturally, I knew that no one could move until the King or Queen moved, and in the end, in desperation I suppose, she dragged me on to the dance floor for a dance. It then dawned on me that what she had been trying to say was would I open the *floor* with her, an old-fashioned English way of asking him to join her in the first dance.'

From Bangkok we flew to Hong Kong, where we stayed at Government House, up in the hills. There was the usual banquet, which was held up for half an hour while Lord Louis tried to sort out the problems of an unfortunate Chinaman who had been instrumental in saving numerous British prisoners-of-war from the Japanese but who could not now get a licence to open his small taxi business. This was so typical of Lord Mountbatten. He was constantly handling similar requests wherever we went in the world, and he always did his utmost to help. Of course, his whole life centred on coping with endless international problems – in particular over defence – but this never stopped him from dealing with the smaller things, like attending a fête to help build a cricket pavilion or village hall, which were so important to the ordinary people he met.

Our next stop was Borneo and Jesselton, where we arrived on the anniversary of Lady Mountbatten's death. We were taken to the house, perched on a small hill in the jungle, in which she had drawn her last breath, the simplest of houses, and the room in which she had died quite peacefully in her sleep, the simplest of rooms. Lord Louis was struck – as we all were – by the plain wooden floor, the small wooden bed, the lack of decoration of any kind. It was being kept, not so much as a shrine as an everlasting memorial. There were always fresh flowers there. Lady Patricia, who accompanied her father, had brought some roses from Broadlands which we planted on the pathway. I left them alone with their thoughts and wandered away into the jungle with mine.

In Borneo, during the Borneo war of the early sixties, Lord

Louis was lodged in the Chief Administrator's house, which was too small to accommodate me as well. My rooms were five hundred yards down a jungle track, just a short stroll, I thought, when it was pointed out to me in daylight. But night falls rapidly in the Borneo jungle, and when I was ready for bed I found myself alone in pitch-darkness with just the glow of a feeble lantern to light my way down the hill and all around me weird jungle noises. Scared as I was, I recalled our brave soldiers who lived and fought in such conditions and had the additional hazards of booby traps and Japanese snipers to cope with. What had I to fear?

Even with the guerrilla snipers and the monsoon conditions and the dashing in and out of helicopters and the leaping across muddy swamps, I know I felt – and I'm sure others did too – that I wished we could have spent more time in the fragrance and tranquillity of Jesselton and the jungles of Sarawak.

Thence we took passage for Australia, calling in at Manila in the Philippines, and Guam, a huge American base used to launch bombers on their missions to Vietnam. Not my favourite place, Guam. After refuelling in Darwin, we continued on to Canberra, where we were pleasantly surprised to be received by the Prime Minister, Robert Menzies. We looked out of the window as we taxied to a halt, and there he was, dear old Sir Robert, who had quite unexpectedly taken the trouble to come to the airport and meet us. It was a great honour.

I made two trips to Australia with Lord Mountbatten, one in 1961, the other in 1965, and I noticed a big difference in those four years. The immigration policy of the early sixties meant that there was a huge influx of immigrants, from Italy and Greece, from Japan and the Philippines, from all over the place. No longer were the new settlers principally malcontents from Britain. The 'old' Australians and New Zealanders, the Anzac boys who fought in the war, still hold a strong allegiance to the Crown and are amongst the proudest and most loyal of Her Majesty's subjects. The new immigrants cannot be expected to share these feelings, and do not.

I also noticed quite a change in the cities we visited. Melbourne had developed into a concrete jungle. Darwin, just a few tin huts when I first saw it in 1961, had become street upon street of vast office blocks. Sydney too had grown enormously. My only regret was that in two visits to Australia I never got to see Alice Springs or Ayers Rock; nor did I have time to snorkel on the Great Barrier Reef in pink pyjamas!

After a busy couple of days in Canberra, we were granted a brief respite. The New Zealand Navy flew us in a big Sunderland flying boat to the Bay of Islands, where we were the guests of the government. This bay is about as far north as it is possible to go and still be in New Zealand, and it is very, very beautiful. There are said to be over a thousand islands and it seemed like we could see them all as we landed at sunset, having glided over from Auckland. It was a holiday in paradise. Two shark-fishing boats had been laid on for us, so we spent two days fishing from Russell Bay, staying at the lovely Otehei Lodge, which nestles amongst the most beautiful and tranquil islands. We had the hotel exclusively to ourselves.

On the first day, Lord Louis caught a huge white shark, a sort of miniature Jaws, which weighed almost 900 lbs. Lord Louis was strapped into a chair and it took him almost seven hours to land it; by the end of that time he had almost drawn blood through his harness. The shark was a real man-eater of which Lord Louis was vastly proud. After it had been winched up, he decided that he would have the teeth made into necklaces for his grand-daughters, Joanna and Amanda. Seventy-eight very smelly teeth were removed from the three rows – in a shark's jaw the bottom rows close like a jack-knife and the top row comes down between them in a pincer movement, which explains how sharks are able to bite off your leg with a single snap. The teeth were each about the size of an old Gillette razor blade and almost as deadly. Then they were strung into necklaces as a lovely surprise for the grand-daughters the following Christmas at Broadlands.

On the second day, I caught a striped marlin swordfish, a mere 287 lbs. I cannot begin to describe the excitement as it glided into the air and I landed it at the second attempt. A group of Maori girls provided us with a beach barbecue of swordfish steaks and some very potent homemade wine. What a magnificent time we had!

After three restful days and nights in New Zealand, we flew

on to Fiji, crossing the International Date Line. We left on a Thursday and arrived in Fiji on the Wednesday, so we went back to Wednesday again. I think that's how it was – it took us ages to adapt to a eight-day week!

In Fiji there was a reception at Government House. After the dinner party, about two hundred little schoolgirls came out to sing for us on the lawn. There was dancing too, but it was the singing that I shall always remember, under the palm trees and the unbelievably starry sky. The night was balmy and the sounds mysterious and haunting.

It was in Fiji that Lord Louis was presented with a genuine grass skirt, and because it was the real thing, it had to be kept damp. Since we were in the middle of a world tour, that meant keeping it in the bath. So wherever we went thereafter, Lord Louis would say to me: 'Don't forget to put the grass skirt in the bath.'

Whenever we arrived at a new venue, he would have his bath first, and the minute he was out, in would go the grass skirt which would be left floating in the water overnight. In the very early morning, when I was frantically trying to get things packed up, my first and most unwelcome duty was to drain off this blasted soggy mass of wet grass which Lord Louis was absolutely determined should be brought home for the children. As if that was not enough of a problem, I had also been given the nose of my swordfish as a souvenir, which had begun to pong. I wrapped it in everything I could lay my hands on and stuck it in the hold. Fortunately, the hold freezes up in an aircraft, but when we defrosted it back in England the stink was almost unendurable. The grass skirt also survived the journey, but was looking extremely sorry for itself by the time we got it home. Sadly, it had turned almost to raffia. After all the trouble it had given us!

From Fiji we visited Christmas and Easter Islands which had been the sites of the British atomic tests. Originally the Woomera rocket range in Australia had been used, but for some reason the testing was moved to Polynesia and specifically Christmas Island. It was like landing on the moon – burnt-out tree stumps, incinerated scrub, a God-forsaken landscape – and this was a quarter of a century after the explosions. I have often wondered whether what we did then was as safe as the authorities claimed.

The American Pacific Sixth Fleet was based in Honolulu, which was our next stop-over. We visited Pearl Harbor, where all those American sailors were enjoying themselves picnicking and having barbecues when the heavens opened and the bombs descended. Seven thousand sailors were killed, battleships sunk, and the harbour devastated. It has been left as it was as a memorial, with the hulls of the sunken battleships sticking starkly up out of the water. There is a flagpole on which the Stars and Stripes flies and every day homage is paid to the flag and the men who died.

From Honolulu, we went to Hawaii where Lord Louis' curiosity had been aroused by Helio, an active volcano, and probably the only one in the world which may be so very closely observed. The name of the volcano is, I think, Hawaiian and means a fierce sun or a fierce fire. At the time of our visit she was mildly active, but she wasn't being too naughty, so it was thought safe enough for us to climb up to the crater. Around this a safety barrier had been erected. We were a large party, including American generals and admirals and the usual crowd of hangers-on who always like to get in on the freebies.

'Come on, come on,' said Lord Louis and leapt over the barrier.

Naturally I followed him, although I glanced apprehensively at the hissing ground, from which spirals of steam were rising.

Alarmed voices were raised: 'Sir, sir, I don't think it's wise to go any further.'

But Lord Louis ignored them, and shouted to me: 'It's quite safe, Evans, come on, come on, and make sure you've got the cameras ready.'

After about a hundred yards, I looked back and there was nobody at all with us, we were the only two silly beggars. The rest of them were not going to cross that barrier for anybody.

Under the ground there was this angry hissing and muttering and you could feel the heat all around you. When we reached the very edge of the crater the sight was unforgettable. It was like looking down 800 feet into a steel furnace or a boiling cauldron; it was quite terrifying. All the time we watched, the sides were shifting and grumbling and falling and I had the feeling that the volcano was saying to us: 'You come one step nearer and I'll get you!'

Lord Louis asked for the cine camera, which I had already loaded with a fresh reel of film. It was a bit antiquated but had a zoom lens which whirred away. Lord Louis got down on all fours and began a sort of commando crawl to get closer to the edge. I grew more and more concerned as I thought, What if the edge crumbles? There would be no chance of rescuing him then. At first I grabbed hold of the tail of his overcoat, but I needed more purchase so I shifted my grip to his ankles. By now his elbows were actually over the edge of the crater and I was hanging on for grim death and digging my heels in, for Lord Louis was quite a heavy man. My knuckles were white, and what with the heat of the ground and the frozen air there was steam all around us. It was like being in the jaws of Hades.

My relief at escaping from that gloomy place was considerable, I can tell you. Lord Louis had been quite oblivious of any danger but I felt myself quietly shaking as we returned to the rest of the company.

From Hawaii we travelled to Acapulco. Lord Louis had not been there since he accompanied the then Prince of Wales on a visit in 1922. He remembered it as being a romantic little fishing village, just a few huts on the beach. Now it was a throbbing city, one of the world's great playgrounds, a den of iniquity. We stayed at a house called Nardos (which translates as the Eagle's Nest). Perched high on a mountain top, it overlooked the whole of Acapulco and the bay. Our hosts were Mr and Mrs Ivor Bryce who were also to welcome us to their house in Nassau. Right below us was Las Brisas, a luxury hotel which boasted that every room had its own swimming-pool. Further down the mountainside, I counted another ninety private pools before my head began to swim. The Bryces had an enormous pool in the centre of their house with a cluster of transplanted palm trees.

Acapulco has the most equable climate. At night all the doors and glass screen windows were left open and everything in the house was completely exposed to the elements, and yet in the morning everything was precisely as it had been – the grand piano, the books, furniture. There was no moisture, and therefore no damage. Merle Oberon had a house in Acapulco which was constructed inside a cave, in which there were bridges decorated with coloured lights. In the drawing-room you could watch the sea lapping round you as you drank your cocktails. This remarkable home was the main attraction and principal watering-hole of the film-star colony.

After San Francisco, where our hosts, the American Navy, had their headquarters right under the Golden Gate Bridge, our journey east took in Omaha, Ottawa and Labrador for refuelling. On the very last leg home, we were unable to land at London because of the fog and were rerouted.

Such an anti-climax to one hell of an unforgettable world tour. I found it hard to credit just how many miles we had travelled and how many fabulous sights we had seen in a mere six weeks.

In 1962 I accompanied Lord Louis on his tour of the West Indies. The Government had asked him to take on the Defence Survey prior to the Commonwealth nations being granted independence. So wherever we went we had meetings with defence chiefs, government and local authority officials. There were night stops throughout the Caribbean. We started from South America – Venezuela – and our first port of call was Trinidad, where we stayed at the Hilton Hotel. It is unlike any other Hilton, and probably unlike any other hotel in the world. You arrive at the main entrance and you think: 'Where is the hotel?' Hiltons are usually envisaged as soaring into the skies. In the Trinidad Hilton, which is built into the side of a mountain, you arrive on the roof and travel down to the ninety-eighth floor.

From Trinidad, we toured the principal Caribbean islands, Antigua, Jamaica, Belize and the Caymans. It almost broke my heart. I would have given my right arm for a swim and a sunbathe on the beach, because those islands had some won-derfully happy memories for me from my early naval days. But a quick dip in the hotel pool was the most we ever had time for – if we were lucky. I vowed then that I would one day take my holidays there, removed from all the pressures, and so I did. In fact, it is to this part of the world, specifically to the southern part of the Windward group, that I hope to retire and spend my twilight years.

There is nothing to touch it. Some islands, and notably many in French Polynesia, are very beautiful but have been plagued for more than a generation with French atomic tests and nuclear blasting grounds. This kind of sacrilege has not yet – God grant it never does – ruined the Caribbean, where the only real danger is the odd hurricane. These are spasmodic, and when a big one does come along, about once every ten years, the damage is never permanent. Left to itself nature is a great healer and left to themselves people are remarkable survivors.

The following year, we toured South America, although in the manner of such things, we started from the Bahamas, where Lord Louis, as Chief of the Defence Staff, was to attend the Nassau Conference of 1963. We were lodged close to the centre of the town with the Bryces in Balcony House, one of the original colonial houses, all wooden lattices. The suites had been designed in highly individual styles and situated around a beautiful tropical garden. Lord Louis was in the Old Slaves' Kitchen; I was next door in the Laundry. The ADC was in the Pantry and the PA was in the Bakery.

One day I noticed an old man staggering from the bar and toddling off to the garden.

'Do you know who that is?' Lord Louis asked me, and of course I didn't. 'That,' he added, 'is Ian Fleming.'

Not that the name meant anything to me at the time, though I gathered later that Mr Bryce was one of the early backers of the Bond films, which may be why Fleming was staying there.

Bond 007 was full of charm and charisma, dashing, daredevil, handsome and all the rest of it. And here was Ian Fleming, his inventor, a dotty-looking character who was in his fifties but appeared to be at least seventy. He was unkempt and sloppy, not at all sociable, and quite lacking in the charm and charisma of his hero. Nor was I particularly impressed when Lord Louis told me that this man was going to be hugely famous with his Bond films. President Kennedy was at the Nassau Conference, and it was Kennedy's announcement that the Bond books were amongst his favourites that caused them to become the fashion in Washington. I wonder if Lord Louis introduced the President to them in Nassau.

The South American tour proper began in Mexico City, where tourists are recommended to spend a few days adjusting to the thin air before going off sightseeing. We had no time for such niceties, so we were followed around by a team of army medics carrying oxygen who gave us an occasional whiff to keep us going. Since the Andes were some 24,000 feet above sea level, this was essential.

We stayed at the Isabella, a large and beautiful hotel right in the heart of the capital, and it was while we were there that I experienced my first earth tremor.

Downtown Mexico City is like the rush-hour traffic jams of Hyde Park Corner, Oxford Street and Piccadilly rolled into one with everyone going in different directions. Wherever we went we were accompanied by a police escort consisting of a motorcade of fifteen policemen on motorbikes in a swan-like V-formation ahead of us and a carload of trained American G-men fore and aft. They were tight on security there and needed to be.

I was in the front of the car as usual, when Lord Louis suddenly shouted to me: 'Do you see the policemen? Do you see what they are doing?'

I looked. Their sirens were blaring and they all had whistles in their mouths, but the most impressive thing was that none of them were holding on to the handlebars of their bikes. Their arms were in front of them as they did a sort of breast stroke in an attempt to clear the traffic. And they succeeded. We passed through that traffic like a dose of salts. When I say the Mexicans are the maddest drivers in the world, I don't exclude the maniacs on the Champs-Elysées. As for the G-men, they had cars with adapted running boards, broad and low to the ground. The driver would of course be in the car, and there would be six men hanging from handles on top, three on each side. The windows were kept open, and, while I watched and wondered, I saw one of the men pull himself up on the handle and slide himself in through the back window –

all in a single movement. Then the next opened the back door and slid in; then the third slithered into the front door as we gathered speed. They were great acrobats and it was great theatre.

Lord Louis was so taken with this display that later he asked for a demonstration. This we were privileged to observe in some side streets, the Mountbatten cine camera hard at work. I could not help wondering what the poor policemen thought of this inquisitive V I P.

A brief visit to Venezuela followed, but we were all looking forward most keenly to Peru, where our schedule allowed us time to see the land of the Incas and Machu Picchu.

To get to Cusco from Lima we had to take an old Dakota belonging to the local airline which appeared to be tied up with string and which bumped and lurched for an hour as we flew up into the Andes. I had always had a dread of crash-landing in the Peruvian Andes and eating the other passengers or being eaten by them and never being seen again; and here I was in this wretched, clapped-out crate which was full of chicken coops and old Indian women wearing bowler hats and carrying cooking pots. We had, I suppose, just about reached the point of no return (about one hour's flying) when the starboard engine sprung a massive oil leak, to which the pilot responded by switching off the engine. The Dakota was not pressurised and we were forced to rely on oxygen tubes. Unfortunately there were no masks and the gas was sucked straight from the tubes, an uncomfortable process since, whatever the oxygen touches – lips or teeth or mouth – it freezes immediately. The sensation was like having your face and mouth attacked by a mad surgeon with a scalpel. All the while, we were bouncing and bumping around these beastly mountains, I was aware of the perspiration tingling on my forehead. To make matters worse, one of the dear old Inca women passed out and went bright blue so there was quite a drama as everyone set about trying to save her life, while hanging on to their own life-saving tubes of oxygen, which hissed like angry snakes.

In Cusco we stayed in a poky and rather dirty little hovel of a hotel which was unused to tourists. So far above sea level the air is extremely thin, even thinner than in Mexico City, and there were huge oxygen cylinders everywhere. The bumf we had been handed kept on insisting that 'it is vitally important that at least four days is given to this venture' and here we were doing it in forty-eight hours, and fitting in Venezuela and Mexico City as well!

The morning after we arrived, we boarded a tiny little funicular train, no more than a single carriage, which shunted its way up the mountainside. First it would go a couple of hundred yards in one direction, then the driver would get out and switch the points, after which it would go a couple of yards in the other direction, zig-zagging ever upwards. It then followed a jungle trail, along one of the narrowest gorges in the world, which had been opened up forty years earlier by Hyram Bingham, the great American explorer. What a brave man he must have been to have ventured so deep into what was then forbidden territory! At intervals along the railway track there were Inca family groups patiently waiting for anything we could throw them. The women, covered with brightly coloured rugs, wore the traditional bowler hats and smoked clay pipes. Some had babies' heads peering over their shoulders. They begged us for a few pesetas or tried to persuade us to buy some rug or hat. There was no sign of human habitation and I could not help wondering just how far these dear people had trekked.

Eventually we came to the base of Machu Picchu, where a battered old bus awaited us to take us up a tiny roadway that had somehow been cut into a steep little pinnacle like a giant anthill. This took us up a further 2,000 feet above sea level. In low gear all the way and after one of the most hair-raising bus rides of my life, the rickety old bus eventually got us to within half a mile of the lost land of the Incas, the Hidden City.

When finally we reached the Hidden City, I was lost in pure amazement. It was quite silent. There was nobody around except a few Inca women with their babies wrapped in shawls. They wore long coats made from llama wool, the best possible protection against the cold. Nor could we see any houses up there. But everywhere there were these huge pillars and slabs of rock, five to six feet high and most beautifully carved. How did they get them there, right up to the very highest peak? There were arches made without any kind of cement, just huge lintels placed over pillars. Such tiny people they must have been, these amazing Incas, because to get through the arches we had to almost double ourselves up. We were in the clouds. All around us, huge, foreboding mountain peaks which have never been climbed and probably never will be. Clouds passed above our heads and below us in the valley. We could just see the gorge and the river running through it like a thread of cotton. And all the time we kept reminding ourselves of Hyram Bingham, quite a young man, a doctor I believe, and of how he must have hacked his way through the jungle to one of the most inaccessible places on earth – the Lost City of the Incas.

Nobody can date this architectural miracle, but it is age-old. For millions of years the hidden tribe of Incas had lived here. The environment could not have been harsher – no fields, no terraces. How could they have grown enough food merely to survive? This Inca city is classed as one of the seven wonders of the world. I would say it is the wonder of all wonders.

From the heights of the Andes we descended to the sea for a rest and a day's shark-fishing. But shark-fishing off the coast of Peru is a long way removed from the Bay of Islands in New Zealand. This is a thoroughly hostile coastline, harsh, dry and hot, and I could well imagine Humphrey Bogart or Ernest Hemingway having a real smash with the bottle there. In fact, the Cabo Blanco club was one of Hemingway's haunts.

We had been provided with the most magnificent boat, and as we were trawling for sharks, a horde of huge, brown, raggedy pelicans came and settled on the water all round our boat and kept us company. We caught no sharks, but we did take a few large tuna. We also worked up a desperate thirst and came away with severe sunburn. We were exhausted after this 'rest'.

Further south, in southern Chile, we stayed in Valparaiso, which is very like the South of France, with palm trees, yacht clubs, exclusive villas and very wealthy people. The most successful of the South American tin miners and ranchers buy large ranches in and around Valparaiso, and it was on one of these estancias that we stayed.

We then moved across the continent to Brazil and the new

capital, Brasilia, a modern wonder of the world, a custom-built city with tower-blocks ten times the size of any you might see in London. This city was built according to the principles of Le Corbusier, the idea being that all the residents would live in vast tower-blocks. Below them would be colonnades with shopping arcades, clinics, schools, theatres, everything the inhabitants could possibly need. Four of these huge skyscraper blocks were built in the desert, and all the surrounding area was landscaped with fountains, lakes and lawns. All the roads leading into this city came in below the level of the landscaped gardens, so traffic was never seen, and yet you could take the train, the bus or your car into the very heart of the capital to park. As for the magnificent Catholic cathedral, this too was partly concealed so that all that could be seen was the spire and the cross. One of the most remarkable of the buildings was the Parliament, designed as an upturned cup and saucer, one for the Government, the other for the Opposition, and the Cup and Saucer is just what the locals called it. But for all its brilliance, I rather got the feeling that the design had not worked, that it was not truly popular with those who lived and worked there. This anthill complex is really not for humans.

In Rio de Janeiro, a Bolivian millionaire laid on for us a miniature version of the Rio Carnival, with dancers and musicians in peacock feathers performing the same routines as in the Carnival proper. It was two in the morning; we had been travelling all day; I had not had time to bath or shave, but I could not resist the crazy and haunting beat of that wonderful Rio music which came drifting into the embassy as I worked away at my lists and papers. It lives with me to this day.

The following morning was for sightseeing and we were taken by car up to the huge statue of Christ on top of Sugar Loaf Mountain. Our host warned us not to take with us anything of value, since we were sure to be robbed. We pointed out that we would be accompanied by security men, but we were told not only that we would get robbed, but where we would be robbed, as well as by whom. We left behind us jewellery, watches, rings and fountain pens, but we each took a little pouch of government money. We were told: 'When you are held up, just hand over these pouches and they'll let you go without slitting your throats.' Apparently the jails were so full that 290 convicted murderers who could not be accommodated had been set free to roam the streets of Rio. Sure enough, halfway up the mountain, out popped the bandits and put guns to our heads. We handed over the pouches and they said: 'Go on, off you go.' I am not sure to this day whether or not it was a put-up job.

In the Argentine we stayed on another glamorous ranch, whose owner specialised in the breeding of miniature horses, which grew to about the size of labrador dogs. One of them was so tiny that I could stand with my legs apart and not even sit on the horse – this little creature could walk right between my legs. Apparently she had produced three perfect miniature foals, like dolls. They had the gentlest natures, too.

We flew home via Montevideo, which was interesting to naval men like Lord Louis and myself, because it is the site of the Battle of the River Plate, when the great German battleship the *Admiral Graf Spee* was trapped by our cruisers, the *Exeter*, the *Ajax* and the *Achilles*, and eventually scuttled outside the harbour in 1939.

Such memories may make it appear that out tours were an endless round of pleasure, banquets and sightseeing, fishing and lying in the sun. For me it was the hardest of hard work and for Lord Louis it meant prolonged and exhausting battles with governments and defence chiefs.

Lord Louis always insisted that I accompany him everywhere, though frequently I could have cried through lack of sleep and sheer mental and physical exhaustion. I could never plan a session of packing without anticipating hearing a familiar shout: 'Come on, Evans, you may never get another chance in your life to see something like this.'

It might be the Persian Crown Jewels, the Kariba Dam, or the Bulawayo copper mines. But it was not just my company he sought. I was also there to make detailed notes of everything: the number of cars in our welcome cavalcade at whatever airport it happened to be – the record was Monrovia where I counted ninety-two – the official explanations, the burden of the speeches, everything, so that in the evening he would be able to dictate his tour diary to his PA whilst dressing. How many bodyguards were there, Evans? What was the general's name, Evans? What was that stuff they showed us at wherever it was? How much of this? How many of that? And, Evans, what *was* the other thing? Remind me to get one for the Queen.

When finally he left, my poor old head would be buzzing, not just from exhaustion, but because there was never, not ever, an opportunity to relax.

But if he had not pushed me to the limit and insisted that I always accompanied him, however would I have managed to see all those miraculous sights? How could I have seen assembled thousands of tribesmen, or witnessed the secret love-in ceremonies of the New Guinea bushmen? Who would have laid salt for me in the African bush to ensure that I saw all those elephants and rhino? Who would have invited me to picnic with the King of Siam, or stay with those film stars? How otherwise could I have visited so many castles, palaces, embassies and royal residences? Would William Evans have had the use of private jets, or met Incas, Mexicans, West Indians, Red Indians, Indian Indians, gauchos, cowboys, Amazonians, Masai, Kikuyu and Kano tribesmen, Eskimos, Mounties, Ashantis, sultans, emirs, presidents, emperors, shahs, kings, queens, princes, princesses, Maoris, Fijians, Tahitians and great world leaders? Would he have had a chance to see almost everything the world has to offer?

Somehow I doubt it.

Chapter Seven:
Gold Teeth, Beatles Wigs and the
Revolution That Never Was

Lord Louis was at his best and happiest at Christmas, and on his tours and travels he was always on the look-out for Christmas presents for his grandchildren. It was a small skirmish in the early days when he had just four or five grandchildren, but as the years passed it became a major military operation, for there were now seven young Knatchbulls and three little Hickses to be catered for. So, wherever we travelled and whatever we found, be it elephant droppings from Africa or sharks' teeth from New Zealand or lava rock from Hawaii, we had to make sure that we had ten of everything. The Christmas stockings which had to be filled with this treasure trove of curiosities were not just your common or garden Christmas stockings either; they were heavy-duty, long, men's shooting stockings, and took a good deal of filling.

I don't suppose any child in the world received such stockings as these children did. In each one there would be over eighty little parcels, and each treasure would be accompanied by a small typed card explaining the details of just what it was and the circumstances in which it had been found. Every present was a lesson in history or geography.

Lord Louis loved to have fun with these gifts. Take the case of the oval-shaped nuts which had passed through the elephants' intestines. These would be wrapped so as to appear box-shaped, and anything box-shaped would be wrapped into the shape of a ball. This added greatly, of course, to the excitement. A lot of the items were insignificant little things, not treasures or jewels. There might be seeds from different parts of Africa, Eskimo carvings from Canada, postcards and mementoes from hotels we had stayed in, special menus and programmes from grand functions, gadgets from Hong Kong, starfish from the South Seas, pieces of coral, shells, almost anything and almost everything.

Some presents posed particular problems. There were, for instance, the multicoloured bird-of-paradise feathers from New Guinea; these had been heavily poached by tourists in the forties and fifties, and even with Lord Louis exerting all his influence we had the greatest difficulty finding and exporting ten sets of them, and making sure that they remained undamaged.

I would start packing these gifts from September onwards at all available moments. I was grateful for Lord Louis' methodical hoarding of old Christmas wrappers and ribbons, because when it came to wrapping ten times eighty little presents, I needed every scrap of paper and cardboard, every loose end of string, every box I could find. I also had to type cards for these 800 gifts. Lord Louis wrapped one or two of the presents, but I did the vast majority of them. I was also responsible for presents for all the family and friends, the staff and the tenants, so you may well imagine the complexity of the operation.

I did not myself receive a stocking for Christmas, but I always got a present, and occasionally it would be something which I would treasure for the rest of my days.

At Broadlands Lord Louis had his own tweed, as the Queen does at Balmoral. The Mountbatten tweed is a pleasant blue and grey, and exclusive to family, close friends and the keepers, who wear it as a kind of livery. Naturally, therefore, to be given a bolt of this cloth was a signal honour, and it was not an honour which was bestowed lightly. A bolt had been given to the Queen, who had skirts made from it which she always wore on her visits to Broadlands. On other Christmases he would give Her Majesty presents connected with her love of horses, a new riding whip or aiguillette for Trooping the Colour, that sort of thing. Prince Philip and Prince Charles had also been given bolts of Mountbatten of Burma tweed.

Just before Christmas one year when I had been organising

the presents as usual, there was one bolt of tweed left unwrapped and I assumed it must be for some personal friend of Lord Louis whom perhaps for some reason he did not want even me to know about. We had checked through all the presents and I brought the bolt to his attention.

'That's all right, Evans, that's all right,' he said, and I wondered why there should be such a mystery, because he was not normally a man to keep things from me, however private. It niggled me slightly because I was never left in the dark, never.

Come Christmas Eve and he wrapped the last few of the special presents himself, presents for his daughters probably, just for the fun of it, but still there was this bundle of tweed left over. He said: 'Leave it, Evans, leave it, I'll wrap it later.'

I still did not know whom it was for.

The next morning it was traditional for all the family to line up in the grand hall in front of the Christmas tree, Lady Patricia and Lord Brabourne, Lady Pamela and Mr David Hicks, and then all the grandchildren – a charming sight. I organised carols on the record player as gentle background music and then announced each member of the staff and tenants until only Charles Smith, the butler, and I were left. Then, from behind Lord Louis' back out came this huge bundle, and immediately I guessed what it must be. A bolt of Broadlands tweed – for me. I knew it was not given lightly, so I was full of pride that I was considered worthy of it; the tears prickled behind my eyes, especially at the cunning way he had bamboozled me over it. I had it made into a shooting suit.

After this ceremony I had to walk down the line of some fourteen or fifteen people, and each one would have a gift for me. Lady Patricia gave me a little painting of Classiebawn, the children gave me socks or a tie or a diary. Something from everyone, ending with the dear twins, Timothy and Nicholas. How could I have possibly imagined that Nicholas would be brutally murdered at just fourteen?

I recall with particular pleasure another occasion. My birthday falls around Trafalgar Day, in October. Each year we would have a little joke. I would say, 'Great day, this, great day', and Lord Louis would grin to himself, affecting to have forgotten, and then say, 'Oh yes, Trafalgar Day, of course. What a great day!'

Sure enough, out in due course would come his very special present, and the most special of all was a pair of Mountbatten cufflinks in a beautiful little box. I still have them, and I treasure them.

As for me, I gave him small but useful things. I had very little money, and he was well aware of that, so I would present him with something special and appropriate, or something simple he really needed, like a new black bowtie. Tapes were always welcome, of his favourite musical, say, *Camelot*, or the *Planet Suite*, or the 'Pomp and Circumstance' marches or the *Goon Show* or *The Navy Lark*, his favourite radio comedy, which we would listen to on the car radio until he almost killed himself laughing at the antics of Petty Officer Pertwee.

In London Lord Louis had a small maisonette in behind Wilton Crescent, Belgravia. After he retired as CDS in 1965, we had moved out of the big house on Wilton Crescent and into what had been the offices at the back. The first floor consisted of a modest drawing-room, a tiny bedroom, bathroom and kitchen; on the second floor were an even tinier bedroom and bathroom for me. The interior design had been put in the hands of David Hicks, Lord Louis' son-in-law, and naturally it was extremely tasteful. Lord Louis was always keen to advance David Hicks's career whenever and wherever he could.

Arriving at the flat by car was always something of an event for us, because the garage door had been fitted with one of Lord Louis' beloved gadgets. A touch of the button in the car and the garage door would swing open; most convenient and in the sixties something of a rarity. Nine times out of ten I would be doing the driving, but it was he who always insisted on pressing the button. No matter how many times he did it, it still charmed and impressed him.

At the big house in Wilton Crescent we did much of our formal entertaining, with lunch parties for military VIPs and NATO chiefs as well as royal relations. But the new maisonette was too small to permit any entertaining on the grand scale, and it was not unusual for me to attend to a couple of kings – Gustav of Sweden and Constantine of Greece – by bringing them sandwiches from the sandwich bar across the

Lord Louis on the steps of
the Ministry of Defence on
relinquishing his last
command as Chief of the
Defence Staff, June 1965

The presentation of
standards in Germany,
representing the Queen
Mother. This was the
second official engagement
of three on the first day of
our supposed holidays.

The sword table, with the Freedom of the City of London sword placed, signifi-cantly, above the Japanese surrender sword

The Green Room at Broadlands, where Nehru meditated

Broadlands. My flat was situated under the long roof at right angles to the main house.

Saturday night at the flicks at the Broadlands 'Regal'. I seemed to know everybody! The Queen is on the extreme left and Charles Smith the butler is sitting on the step in front of me.

The Duke and Duchess of Windsor's arrival at Southampton on their only post-Abdication visit to England, to unveil a memorial to Queen Mary. I'm on the far left of the picture and Mountbatten's famous silver mascot can be seen on the Zephyr Zodiac to the right.

Classiebawn Castle

Lord Louis directing the mooring of *Shadow V*. I'm the one doing all the work.

Sharing the spoils on
Shadow V, Mullaghmore
harbour

Granddaughter Joanna
being told to hurry up by
Grandpa on a prawning
expedition

Shadow V coming up to the lobster-pots, as she would have been doing on that fatal day in August

The Duke of Westminster's yacht, *Trasna of Ely*, on which I spent my last day with Mountbatten, four days before the tragedy

street or a few prawns from the fridge, before taking in a theatre. I remember one occasion when the American ambassador called, but, because there were two kings in the drawing-room, he had to sit on Lord Louis' bed while there was an admiral sitting on my little stool in the kitchen awaiting an important meeting. With so many callers and so little room in which to receive them, one had to learn to be very diplomatic at times. It does not come naturally to ask ambassadors whether they would mind waiting in the bedroom or admirals to perch in the kitchen.

Lord Louis loved the theatre. Musicals in general, and *Camelot* in particular appealed to him. What he always enjoyed was arranging to take the Queen privately to see a brand-new show. Together they attended various premieres, of course, but to go informally was so much more pleasant. Her Majesty's diary was easily as full as Lord Louis', but once or twice a year they would synchronise their evenings for a private outing, usually when Prince Philip was abroad. I would book the tickets in my name.

Lord Louis adored Her Majesty and always had done. He was also virtually a father to Prince Philip, because, after the death of his own father, Philip had lived with the Mountbattens and had even taken their name. Lord Louis used to claim – half in earnest, perhaps – that for several months the Mountbattens were on the throne of England. Those were the months between the accession of Her Majesty and the Coronation, because, according to the law of England, until she was crowned, Her Majesty took the name of her husband and would have been, whether she liked it or not, Mrs Mountbatten, just as Princess Anne is Mrs Mark Phillips.

It has sometimes been said that Lord Louis masterminded the marriage between Her Majesty and Prince Philip, but one must not forget that Princess Elizabeth was only thirteen when she first set eyes on the strikingly handsome young officer from Dartmouth Naval College and became understandably besotted with him. But it was not just a teenage crush. Lord Louis idolised the young princesses, who used to come and stay with him in Malta, and quite apart from dynastic considerations it was a match which clearly must

119

have pleased him mightily. It was natural, too, that he should have been asked to become godfather to their firstborn child.

At that time, the Royal Family was a bit short of senior male members; indeed, it still is. And Lord Louis was not only the grandfather of the family, but clearly the man with the greatest experience of the world and all its ways. The old Duke of Gloucester was very ill, and the other royal dukes extremely young, a different generation.

Lord Louis would have been delighted if his grand-daughter, Amanda, had married Prince Charles. They were second cousins, as are the Queen and Prince Philip. They had grown up together and were great friends, nothing more, just brotherly and sisterly. In 1979 he had arranged to take his godson and his grand-daughter to India with him, but Prince Philip opposed the arrangements, feeling that his son would be upstaged in India by the legendary figure of Mountbatten, and I believe that this assessment was correct, for, though the Indians would adore Prince Charles, Mountbatten will for ever be very special to them.

There are those who argue with assumed authority that, if Lord Louis had still been with us, perhaps Prince Charles might not have married Lady Diana Spencer. What I do know is that he would have thoroughly approved of the girl Prince Charles did choose – and that he would have been enchanted with her. The Princess of Wales is everything Lord Louis admired in a woman, beautiful, fair, tall and elegant, and it is certain that the old boy would have fallen in love with her, as indeed most of us did. Clearly the Princess of Wales still has a good deal of experience to gain, but it is no easy thing to become a member of the Royal Family overnight. If you are not to the manner born, it takes a good deal of hard work, and it must have been a very great burden for a girl as young as the Princess was when she married. Had he survived, Lord Louis would have been able to help her a great deal, I am sure, and would have advised her on protocol and royal procedures.

Together they would have created a magnificent coalition of fun, friendship and love and I am sure the Princess would have been wholly enchanted by Lord Louis.

The Court has changed. The Prince is surrounded by young equerries, and few of the grand old boffins remain to advise him, noblemen who have been in the family for generations, who advised the late King, who know the royal procedure. Prince Charles belongs in the modern world, and amongst his staff are industrialists and whizzkids. That would have been unheard of a generation back. Change has come to the Royal Household. Is it progress or just the way of the world? Is it for the best?

Prince Charles and Lord Louis were always very close. They shared polo week-ends, they shot grouse at Balmoral and pheasants at Sandringham together. In due course, Prince Charles came to look on Broadlands as his second home. He would motor up from Portsmouth when he had his ship *Bronnington*, a minesweeper and one of the Royal Navy's smallest ships, there.

I can observe many of Lord Louis' mannerisms in Prince Charles. When he talks to people with a forefinger out, pointing at the face, head tilted, that is Mountbatten. It has often been remarked that Prince Charles walks with his hands behind his back just like his father, but that too is a Mountbatten characteristic. So is the quiet, striding, half-marching walk and the hand in the pocket with the thumb out. Even the profile is beginning to take on the same bearing.

Three Wilton Crescent was the London base for our 'premiere banquets', dinners given before or after the various film premieres which Lord Louis so enjoyed giving. After Lady Louis' death, and the setting up of the Edwina Mountbatten of Burma Memorial Trust, I remember after one such banquet during the winter of 1961 escorting Audrey Hepburn, the star of the chosen film, to her car at about two in the morning. It was an icy night, and the pavement was slippery, so she grasped me tightly by the arm – really gripped me – and said: 'Don't let me go, will you, Evans?'

And she put her arm in mine and I held her tight. She was very small and delicate.

There we both were walking up Wilton Crescent in the middle of the night with her shivering and holding on to me and saying: 'Don't let me slip, will you?'

And I replied: 'I wouldn't let you go for the world.'

I could hardly believe it, that here I was, arm in arm with

the girl I had fallen so passionately for in *The Nun's Story*, walking her down the grey streets of London, and she just as lovely as ever! I was on Cloud Nine.

Another notable guest for another notable premiere was Maria Callas, the famous opera diva. On the way to her car she invited Lord Louis to join her for a cruise on Aristotle Onassis's magnificent yacht. Yes, he said, he would certainly make time for that, but added, nodding in my direction, that his Chief Petty Officer Evans would have to accompany him; whereupon she smiled at me and said that I would be more than welcome and she would greatly look forward to seeing us both. Sadly, she fell out of favour with Onassis before the invitation could be fulfilled, much to our loss, I am sure, as the *Christina* was a truly magnificent yacht.

I was once due to collect Lord Louis from a film premiere at the Odeon in Leicester Square, and we were scheduled to drive straight off to visit the Atlantic College in Wales. This was the first United World College, which Lord Louis had helped to found and the presidency of which he was to hand over to Prince Charles. My instructions were to have the car ready to do an immediate bunk as soon as Lord Louis had said good-bye to Her Majesty, and to have our Jaguar directly behind the royal car.

Cars were ordered to be at the cinema at 11.15 p.m. and with ten minutes to go I arrived at Leicester Square to find it packed solid with the huge limousines of all the great folk attending the premiere. I had been so busy closing down the flat and packing that I had had no time to waste sitting in Leicester Square for hours. I was in the sleek little two-toned Jaguar with its silver mascot, and no sooner did I get close to the Odeon than I was surrounded by police superintendents and inspectors screaming: 'Get this car out of the way, get this car out of the square!' while the crowd, a little fractious after waiting so long for royals and film stars to emerge, laughed and whistled and hissed.

I quietly climbed out of the car and screwed on the Royal Shield, a gold crown on a red background. Immediately all the superintendents and inspectors turned to all the other big Rolls-Royces and limousines and started screaming at them instead. A great cheer went up from the packed square.

Lord Louis' love for the cinema and cinema people went back a long way. He made his first Hollywood picture in 1922 while spending part of his honeymoon at Pickfair, the home of Douglas Fairbanks Snr and Mary Pickford in Hollywood. The film was a home movie and involved the participation of the young Charles Chaplin who announced bluntly to him, 'You ain't no actor.' During the thirties Lord Louis campaigned for the showing of talking pictures on board naval ships at sea, sending Noël Coward to find out what sort of films the men would like to see and being disappointed to find that they preferred unpretentious British films to his own taste for American westerns and war films. This early initiative resulted in the founding of the Cinematographic Society, which took films to the troops, and the formation of the Royal Naval Film Corporation, which brought films on to naval ships for the first time, for which the film industry in general was forever grateful to him.

Lord Brabourne, Lord Louis' son-in-law, is a film producer, and one of his films was a sort of *Mutiny on the Bounty* called *HMS Defiant*. Alec Guinness played the captain and Dirk Bogarde, his first lieutenant. When we visited the set, it was my first sight of the making of a film. There was this huge stern of a ship, something like the old *Victory*, built in the studio, in front of a most unimpressive-looking backcloth. I thought that this was nothing like a man-of-war drifting in a fog at night off the French coast and said to Lord Brabourne: 'You'll never get away with this. It's nothing like a sea scene.'

'Just you wait until you see the film,' he replied.

I did. Alec Guinness was standing on deck and a dead Dirk Bogarde was hanging over the handrail. Guinness finished making a speech and crossed over to slash the handrail with his sword and hurl Bogarde into the sea. While it was being shot it was bathed in brilliant lighting, a smoke bomb had just been let off and a little man was waving a fan to make the smoke drift about and appear like fog. The camera was mounted on a tilting mechanism that made it seem as though the ship was pitching and rolling. Little Johnny Briggs, Mike Baldwin in *Coronation Street*, was there as a young pirate with a headband and a single earring. I had to admit that Lord Brabourne was right!

While the carpenters were adjusting the set, Lord Brabourne said to us: 'If you go through that little door there, you will see them making another film next door.'

We did, and found ourselves in a very different milieu. Strapped to a chair in what was clearly intended to be a spaceship was Bob Hope. I gathered that it should have been a monkey in the chair, because milk and bananas were being fed to Bob Hope down an automatic feeder. Then the mechanism went wrong and Hope kept getting an earful of banana and a faceful of milk. Bing Crosby was sitting and watching, which gave us an opportunity to chat. What a joy to talk to two such great characters, and all so entirely unexpected. Both these great actors were as funny off set and we all had a great time, albeit for only ten minutes. Bing Crosby was in tears like the rest of us at Bob Hope's reaction to this crazy scene.

The Hollywood set threw a big party for Lord Louis at the Beverly Hills Hotel. Clark Gable, Cary Grant, Stewart Granger, all the top actors and all the most beautiful women, everyone was assembled to pay tribute to him. Clark Gable and Cary Grant argued over who should sit next to him on the top table. We left for the function from Mike Frankovitch's house and Claudia Cardinale was in the car. I had to lean in and tuck her beautiful gown clear of the door and around her feet. She gazed down on me with that beautiful look, and it absolutely melted me into the ground – she was barely twenty and so stunning.

This may be the moment to mention that, despite the reputation many of the top film actresses have of being 'painted with the wrong brush', i.e. a little dumb, this has certainly not been borne out by my experience. Shirley Maclaine, who became a great friend of us all, and Princess Grace, with whom I had been hopelessly in love since seeing *High Society*, are – and in the latter case sadly were – women of high intelligence, and wonderful company.

It was in Mike Frankovitch's house that I slept in the most remarkable bedroom of all, more remarkable than my Treetops bunk with the padded tree branch growing across my chest, more remarkable even than my bedroom in the Lutyens-designed Viceregal Palace in Delhi. Lord Louis had been shown to his suite, which was sumptuous by any standards, and he then asked his host – as he always did – where I would be sleeping. Mr Frankovitch took us along a corridor to the cinema, explaining to me that since the house was not all that large, he hoped I would not mind 'camping out' in the cinema. At which he took us into this huge circular room, the size of a small ballroom, with curved windows filling two-thirds of the wall space. Beyond the windows was a white balustraded terrace with a deliciously inviting swimming-pool, and below a panoramic view of Hollywood and the surrounding area. Within the cinema was a raised platform, on which was a cocktail bar and some generously proportioned armchairs. As we watched, Mr Frankovitch pressed a series of switches and before our eyes huge panels descended from the ceiling, hiding the platform and the chairs. The bar slid into a recess in the wall and disappeared, and an enormous circular bed emerged. Meanwhile, the vast windows were covered by curtains which silently closed. It was like being the star of a forties Hollywood film. Lord Louis grinned and asked why had he not been given the cinema; he much preferred it. He was sure that I wouldn't mind a camp bed! But of course what he was after was the opportunity to play with all the gadgets. I am sure he would have spent the night pressing buttons and watching the bar disappear.

One incident of national significance at which I was present took place in May 1968. Cecil King, the Robert Maxwell of his day, had written to Lord Louis requesting a meeting. He turned up at 2 Kinnerton Street for the arranged meeting but after the two men had been together for no more than three or four minutes, Lord Louis came dashing out to the bedroom where I was working and said: 'This man is insane – he wants *me* to organise a coup, throw out the Government and worse, put armed troops on the street. Unbelievable. Me? Put machine-guns on the street? Me? Overthrow the Crown? *Me?* Give me about two or three minutes and then come in and get rid of him.'

This was our usual system with unwelcome guests. After I came in, I would gently mutter, but just loud enough for the guest to hear, that we were required urgently at the Ministry of Defence.

This time I repeated the rigmarole and Lord Louis added to Cecil King: 'Sorry, old bean, but I've got to fly off to the Ministry. Can you return tomorrow and we'll continue this chat then?'

The next day, Lord Louis brought in Solly Zuckermann, his chief scientist and a long-standing personal friend, and Hugh Cudlipp, employed by King but a loyal ally of Lord Louis'.

After a quarter of an hour or so, Sir Solly went storming off, warning Mountbatten to have nothing to do with King; Cudlipp and King left together a little later, looking, I thought, very glum. I was not privy to this meeting, but it certainly left Lord Louis pretty flabbergasted. He found it all too incredible.

I thought nothing more about it until stories began circulating in the press that there had been a plan by Cecil King to overthrow the government of Harold Wilson, and that he had approached Mountbatten as one of the few men in the country with the organising ability to carry such a hare-brained scheme through, and one of the few men with the authority to carry the country with him. A woman very close to the Prime Minister claimed to have evidence that Lord Louis had a map of London with machine-gun emplacements marked on it and that he was behind the planned coup. I can categorically state that nothing could be further from the truth. Of course Lord Louis would have been able to organise just about any task put before him, but he would have been the last man in the world to go along with this madness.

The whole thing was a fantasy of Cecil King's, and he could not have picked a less suitable co-conspirator than Lord Louis, whose loyalty to Crown and country could not have been stronger, and whose respect for democratic principles was profound. Solly Zuckermann had been a great support when the Unified Defence System was being formed; he was a trusted colleague and a great chum. It was Lord Louis' first impression that King had gone nuts. It was clear that Cudlipp, though employed by King, had no great love for the scheme either.

If there remained any doubts about Lord Louis' loyalty to his Prime Minister, they were surely laid to rest when he noted, after Harold Wilson's resignation, that as Prime Minister Wilson had done a good job for the country and saved the economic situation. Indeed, throughout Wilson's premiership, Lord Louis had consistently maintained a considerable respect for his abilities and liked him personally. The PM came round to see Lord Louis privately that evening – no doubt to get a first-hand account of the drama.

Mountbatten was loyal not only to his Queen, his country and his friends, but to his small entourage as well. As a young man he had read Maurice Maeterlinck's *The Life of the Bee*, and it had made a huge impression on him, so much so that all his working life he made what he called 'The Spirit of the Hive' his working philosophy.

Whenever he had to make a decision he involved everyone, taking advice from all of us, and then made up his own mind on the basis of what he had heard. And this philosophy he employed in all things, whether it was planning the highest defence strategy or a Broadlands week-end. In planning world tours the entire entourage was kept informed at every stage of the planning. That way, if somebody fell ill, there was always a substitute ready primed to cover for him, and if there was a flaw in the planning, then several of us had the chance to put it right before it was too late. Consequently, we rarely had any dramas that we could not immediately cope with.

Lord Louis gave the impression of fair-mindedness at all times and would quite often accept advice, though rarely from those with whose opinions he disagreed. He confessed freely that he liked to think that he was almost always right. If this is vanity, he was vain, but then he *was* right – most of the time.

When Roy Jenkins asked him in 1966 to report into prison security after the defection of the convicted spy George Blake, he did so with characteristic energy, canvassing opinions from all sides and at all levels. He asked convicted murderers and lifers how *they* would go about escaping and picked the brains of prison warders, prison governors, chief constables, policemen, and even civilians living near prisons. He visited most of the major penal establishments and, as a result of what he learned, recommended, amongst many other things, that all exercise yards should have obstructive coverings to prevent helicopter lift-offs. Such an eccentric proposal was laughed out of court, but Lord Louis had the last laugh when just such an escape was successfully mounted in Northern Ireland. There have been several others since.

He was just as comprehensive in his researches while conducting the Commonwealth Immigration Commission for the Government. His recommendations on this occasion included curtailing the free immigration of some relatives and dependants from some countries, but again many of these proposals were ignored.

Many years ago, he suggested an underground rail link direct to Heathrow Airport. At the time the idea was considered quite unnecessary. Years later it was brought into being at astronomical cost.

When he was Supreme Allied Commander South-east Asia and responsible for over a million square miles of the world's most hostile territory, he demanded top medical scientists to serve on his staff. There was as usual opposition to such a novel idea, but with malaria, mosquitoes and other tropical diseases accounting for ten times as many casualties at the beginning of the war as enemy action, the best available medical advice was essential. By V J Day, the figures were reversed: for every ten men brought down by the Japanese, only one was incapacitated by disease.

He was always quick off the mark to congratulate and to thank those with whom he had shared successes. I have heard him insist to the Minister of Defence: 'Now, don't forget that this was your idea, no mention of my involvement,' when I knew that the credit should have been his own.

Often he would beat the gun by dictating letters of congratulation before it was quite clear (to me, at any rate) that congratulations were in order. If he was aware that anyone was trying to make up his mind for him, he would deliberately and perversely do the opposite, so one had to be tactful in handling him.

When, for example, my flat at Broadlands was being refurbished, I expressed a preference for a pale blue bathroom suite. He was agreeable to my ordering the colour of my choice, but insisted that I pay for it, as he could not possibly afford, he said, to have all his tenants insisting on their dream bathrooms. Demanding 'full payment', he held out his hand and I popped a shilling (the Queen's Shilling) into it, which satisfied him completely. This incident tool place in front of Princess Alexandra and much notice was taken of the fact that 'CPO Evans has now paid in full for his blue bath.'

Yes, of course he was vain! He was vain about his figure, but he worked hard to keep in trim. He was vain about having retained most of his own teeth, and when he had fillings he preferred gold ones, which regularly fell out, especially when he was indulging his weakness for chocolates and toffees. Nothing pleased him more than to see his photograph on a huge hoarding by the side of the road welcoming him to Monrovia. This caused him to squeeze his hands together and grimace in delight. He was vain about his appearance when he was all dressed up with his Garter Sash and diamond stars, and well he might have been. He certainly seemed to gain at least three inches in height when in full fig. And he was vain when women showed themselves susceptible to him. A very human form of vanity.

With experience, I learned to anticipate Lord Louis' whims, and was able to get him to agree to do almost everything that we wanted him to do; but he had to believe that he had thought of it first. Often I paved the way for others with difficult problems by knowing just what to ask for, when to ask for it, and how to phrase the request.

I can only recall one occasion on which I failed. I had hoped to get the Beatles, then at the height of their fame, invited to Broadlands. I stupidly remarked that they had been to tea with Field Marshal Montgomery, which at once determined Lord Louis *not* to have them. Despite this setback, I was instructed one Christmas Eve to get Lord Louis a Beatles wig, which he was determined to wear at the Christmas party. I had to search the world for such a thing, until eventually one of the directors of the company which produced them drove down specially to Broadlands with one. Lord Louis then wore it for the rest of the day. I wish I could describe what he looked like in it. The best I can do is to say that he looked neither like the Beatles nor like Lord Louis.

He had his own technique for getting his own way with people of consequence. He would begin in a light-hearted, almost frivolous manner, using all the considerable charm at his command, and then suddenly, when the defences were down – Bang! It always seemed to work, but after a particularly trying interview he would emerge smiling and say to me: 'Gosh, that was a tough one!'

He squeezed his hands together and grimaced as though in great pain. Those who knew him well realised that this was an unmistakable sign that he was tickled pink and very highly delighted. This characteristic mannerism gave me anxious moments if he was driving the car at the time! But he was quite unable to suppress his glee, taking both hands off the steering wheel.

There were times when I was under a good deal of pressure, and, being human, I showed it. Normally, I am a bouncing sort and we would have a lot of fun together. I would often break the ice with some silly remark that would make everyone laugh. That is my way. But when things get me down I go very quiet and glum. On such occasions Lord Louis would try to draw me out, and, since it often happened when I was driving him somewhere in the car, he had a particular technique. He would rummage around amongst the tapes and select one which was my favourite, one which soothed me and relaxed me, and he, the Admiral of the Fleet, would slide it into the machine for his Chief Petty Officer. I soon came round.

When he was under pressure he would just shout and bawl on the telephone, and then suddenly explain: 'Don't worry. I know I'm a bit eccentric but I've got to take it out on somebody.' And he was always generous in his apologies when he had let off steam to members of his staff.

He would never expect anyone to do anything he was not prepared to do himself, but he did not suffer fools gladly. After one of his tantrums he would start to laugh and we would all start to laugh, and things would be all right again. This laughter was his safety valve in highly sensitive and tense situations.

A typical scene: we are at the flat and we are going to be late for an appointment and I am in the kitchenette cooking him breakfast. He comes in still in his dressing-gown and starts making the toast, at the same time as rehearsing his speech with much puffing and blowing. It was always like that, a constant whirr of excitement, a constant build-up of pressure.

He would exercise first thing in the morning, the only time available to him. Lying flat on his back he would raise his legs and fling his arms about, puffing heavily. His bathwater had to be checked with a big wooden bath thermometer, and, when the temperature was precisely as he liked it, he would climb in and submerge himself completely, holding his nose as he did so. He would also wash his hair while bathing, which saved time. 'No man is a saint to his valet' runs the old saying, and I subscribe to that! Typically, he would brush his teeth with an electric toothbrush and shave with an electric razor, a patent Ronson model with a built-in battery-charger, while lying flat on his bed to relax his body, dictating letters. Even the PA sometimes had to sit on the loo while Lord Louis had his bath, taking final amendments for an urgent draft. Modesty and nudity took no place in our hectic life!

Once, on a big military tour, he burst into his bedroom ready for a quick change and, flinging off his soiled uniform, flopped on to the bed. Grabbing his razor he started shaving and blurted out to me: 'By the way, I've sold them the missile system. Aren't you impressed?'

'Not especially,' I replied.

'Ah, you will be, though! I've sold them the three ships to fire the missiles from as well.'

I had to confess then that I was a little impressed.

At the dinner party at the embassy that same evening he fixed a deal to sell 280 British Leyland buses, a complete transport system, to a South American city, and sent off a cable to Lord Rootes, clinching the deal there and then.

Our whole life was lived as though there was not a moment to be lost, especially in those first few years after Lady Louis' sad demise. But all living moments were precious.

I prepared the first dress of the day before taking Kelly the labrador out for his ablutions. Then I laid out Lord Louis' breakfast, with such extra treats as the first green figs, ripe peaches, mulberries or raspberries, bringing it from the kitchen in time for the first pips of the main eight o'clock radio news bulletin. After the weather forecast, the radio was switched off, and for some fifteen minutes he would deal with his correspondence, sorting all the letters into Bring-Up Folders (pink), Speech Folders (red), Military Folders (green), and Personal Folders (blue).

Our schedules were always extremely tight, so the timing would be worked out backwards. That is to say, if we were due at a function at eight p.m., we would estimate it would take two hours to drive there, allow twelve minutes to bath and change – that means twelve minutes to eight less two hours – so we leave at ten to six, except that we probably leave at eight minutes to six, and no time had been allocated for me to unload the car and prepare his clothes, which might well be a full ceremonial naval ball dress.

My only resource was to have everything as ready as possible in the hanging wardrobe, so that, when I unzipped it, there would be the uniform with the gold lace trousers, there the glittering diamond stars, there the dress waistcoat with the Garter Sash, there the neck decorations ready with their press studs. The throat tablets and the indigestion tablets would be loaded in the pockets, along with the speech cards in order, the comb on a clip and the ten shillings in five two-shilling pieces to tip the doorman or to get a cab in case something went wrong with the car.

If the function did not involve eating we would have a bag of plums or cherries in the car. I'm sure that sometimes he must have got out of the car to shake hands with some important dignitary and left them with a handful of cherry stones or half-sucked plums. And everyone would be amazed at how quickly he could be got ready. But I always wondered: was all that really necessary? Surely to goodness they would have cheerfully waited an extra five minutes for him.

Chapter Eight:
The Big Man of Queenie

There was so much travelling, so many tours, that my mind is filled with a collage of images. Hotels, palaces, aeroplanes, peoples, luggage, speeches, receptions and uniforms, uniforms, uniforms. Was there a place of any consequence we did not visit, a person of any international standing we did not meet? Sometimes it seemed that we had been everywhere, met everyone and seen everything. How I longed for just a few quiet days at home in Broadlands.

Moorea, just off Tahiti, is one of the most romantic places in the world, a tropical island dream. On the 1965 world tour we stayed in a French hotel on Cooks Bay. It appeared to be little more than a cluster of round, thatched cottages, set amidst waving palms, but offered us every luxury. The main body of the party had been left on Tahiti, and our small entourage was attended by about thirty beautiful young Polynesians wearing cotton shirts and shorts with floral leis in their hair. Across the bay was a breathtaking view of the mountains which represented Bali Hai in the film of *South Pacific*. Luxury and solitude, the best of both worlds. It was while we were at Moorea that the funeral of Queen Louise of Sweden, Lord Louis' sister, took place in Sweden. With some difficulty Lord Louis had managed to contact King Gustav from New Zealand, who insisted that we were not to interrupt our tour for the funeral.

'Queen Louise would not have wanted that,' he said.

In any case it would have been almost impossible for us to have made the trip in time.

Lord Louis and Lady Patricia climbed the hill to a charming little church and said prayers privately there at the same time as the funeral was being held. I felt how much more suitable that was than a panic-ridden dash back to Sweden and the cancellation of so many long-standing commitments across the world.

I liked to think that after so much experience of Lord Louis' ways, nothing could catch me unprepared. But on a cloudless South Pacific dream island I must confess to having been *slightly* wobbled when in the middle of the morning the great man demanded a pair of pyjamas. We were about to go snorkelling on the reef and colourful flimsy shorts and flower leis were the dress of the day. After a moment's thought, I selected the pretty conch-pink pair on the principle that, if he wanted to stand out from the rest of us, he might as well do so in style! We all had to suppress a chuckle as he waded out on the reef in pretty pink P Js with snorkel, mask and flippers, looking like some strange monster from the deep. The rest of the day was spent happily investigating the giant rays and fascinating submarine life of the coral reef and enjoying a delicious picnic. Needless to say, the next morning he was the only one laughing as the rest of us were severely sunscorched and had been burned on the backs of our legs and arms through the water. Next time I go snorkelling I hope I have the courage and, indeed, the good sense to wear pyjamas.

On the last night of our stay on Moorea we attended a traditional Hawaiian-style feast amongst the palm trees. Suckling pigs had been wrapped in banana leaves and cooked on hot rocks in a pit in the ground all day with yams and other delicacies. At sunset there were drinks, followed by a ceremony of opening the oven at which a prayer was offered to the gods for the earth's bounty. Then there was singing and hula-dancing and the pit was opened to reveal the food, which we ate with our fingers out of leaves and shells, drinking from a coconut shell and sitting cross-legged on the ground, our circle illuminated by flaming torches. It was a magical evening tinged with sadness as we remembered our dear Queen Louise.

This was the only occasion on which we changed our programme and extended our stay by two days, abandoning our trip to Bora Bora, which we explained to Lord Louis would be far too boring! As we sailed away from Moorea we flung our flower leis into the water to guarantee our return, one day!

This was the first of only two occasions on which I saw Lord Louis shed tears. The other was when I left his service and we said our goodbyes.

In Greece, King Constantine – Tino to his friends – flew us from Athens to Delphi and took us round the site of the original Olympic Games. I was surprised to find that it was a straight course, not a circular or oval one, and, although all that now remains is an organised ruin, I was filled with a powerful awareness of great athletes from centuries past and felt privileged to breathe in such memories.

There were about fifteen in our party and the King lined us all up, including the ladies. We then did our best running along the ancient course and all managed at least to finish the race. The winner was one of our WRAC stenographers.

One of Lord Louis' unusual duties was to open a small jungle airstrip in the north of New Guinea near Mount Hagen. This had been cut out of the jungle in an area where the tribes were still head-hunting. They had heard about Lord Louis' arrival and referred to him in pidgin English as Big Man of Queenie. He decided to wear a khaki uniform bush jacket, suitable in the heat and the dust, rather than the full ceremonial whites, which he felt might be overpowering.

We were flown in by an Australian bushpilot in a small Piper aircraft and were accompanied by a huge Irish–Australian police commissioner who helped to allay my apprehensions. News travels fast in the jungle and by the time we touched down an estimated 70,000 tribesmen had forgathered. Many of them had walked for weeks to be present and it would take them weeks to walk home, so they were clearly determined to make the most of it. They were more or less naked, splendidly painted, wearing only a few twig things here and there, and were singing, dancing and wailing. Entirely unfamiliar with white men, they looked at me in my blue linen jacket and white trilby most peculiarly, I thought. Was it just my odd clothes or my succulent young body they fancied for dinner?

Lord Louis was presented with a large wand made up of bird-of-paradise feathers, not unlike the Prince of Wales insignia.

'What the hell can I do with this?' muttered Lord Louis. 'I can't ponce about holding it all day long.'

I answered: 'You can't *not* wear it. Look at them all. They are all wearing one.' Some had single feathers, others – the chiefs – a mass of feathers on their heads. The number of feathers indicated their status in the tribe. 'Why don't you put them in your cap?'

He reluctantly agreed and I tucked the feathers down behind his cap badge to make them secure. He looked good. A great roar went up from the 70,000 tribesmen, and it seemed they were thrilled to pieces. It made their day. Then, as he stood on a dais to declare the airstrip open, Lord Louis asked me to film him amongst these New Guinea natives.

'Are you quite sure?' I asked. 'There are some awfully funny-looking people. And the women are smothered in pig grease.'

The grease was rancid and reeking and I felt quite sick with the awful smell of bodies and grease in the overpowering humidity.

None the less, off I trotted with his cine camera whirring, getting strange looks from these tiny head-hunters, who believed, I suppose, that my camera was some kind of weapon. The more old-fashioned their looks became, the more I determined to get away from them before I ended up as somebody's dinner – I could already feel the pinch of salt!

Later, delighted at still being uneaten, we were privileged to watch a special ceremony which, according to the police commissioner, white people were never allowed to see. A long bamboo hut was constructed in the jungle clearing and the old women of the tribes lit fires which filled the interior with smoke. The scent was heady and it seemed certain that some sort of drug was involved. Then the love-in ceremony took place. The engaged couples sat in twos, facing each other on the floor up both sides of the long hut, at the end of which were the girls with bongo drums. The beat at first was a very slow one, while the older women stoked up the fires and chanted. One of the engaged men was all wizened and dried up and appeared to me to be about seventy or eighty.

I said to the commissioner: 'That's a dirty old man with that very young girl. She only looks about twelve.'

But the commissioner put me right. The man's age was probably no more than twenty-five or twenty-six.

'Their life expectancy is very low,' he continued. 'Probably no more than forty for most of them. They marry very young. The couples sit here all night, rubbing noses, while the beat of the drums quickens. Finally they collapse in a trance, possibly from the effects of the drug. Then they go off married into the jungle. And that's the love-in ceremony, which no other white people are known to have witnessed.'

Two or three times a year, we would visit India, stopping off en route at Aden, where there was a large military garrison in the early 1960s. At the time of the Yemenite troubles a lot of British soldiers were being killed and we could take no chances with security. From the moment our jet landed we were surrounded by tanks and armoured cars with armed troops on the tops of nearby buildings.

All traffic in the town was brought to a standstill as we were accompanied by an imposing military escort. On one occasion just before we entered the compound, which included the Governor's house where we were being put up for the night, Lord Louis turned to the escort commander and asked: 'Where can one get transistor radios?'

'In the casbah, sir,' said our young officer in command of the guard.

'Is it far?'

'No, sir. We are about to pass it here on the left.'

'Stop the convoy,' ordered Lord Louis, to the great concern of everyone.

Then three of us, Solly Zuckermann, Lord Louis and I, all in military uniform, left the convoy and made at once for the casbah and the first tranny shop we could find. There we bought a huge box of some two dozen of the cheapest radios that money could buy – less than a pound each. The reason for this detour was that I had received a letter from one of the boys in India, a footman at the palace – he had addressed it, I remember, to 'Bill Mountbatten, England' and the Post Office had delivered it directly to us – in which he begged us to bring transistor radios with us on our next visit. 'They used to want to get to England above all else,' Mountbatten explained. 'Now what they want is to get a transistor. It's their way of learning.'

However excellent his motives, Lord Louis certainly managed to cause great chaos in Aden that morning by bringing a whole military convoy to a halt while he went and bought a box of cheap radios. But I cannot describe the pleasure we gave to the *khidmutgars* (footmen) at Rashtraphati Bhavan.

Dear Pandit Nehru used to say to us at Broadlands that when the electric light came to India it greatly reduced the birth rate, and they were praying for television to arrive to reduce it further, since India has the hopeless task of trying to feed about one-fifth of the world's population and most of them are already in the direst poverty.

In Delhi, Lord Louis had this old barber who used to come and shave him every morning. He was a wizened, white-bearded Indian, a charming old fellow in his eighties. He it was who taught me the yoga techniques of relaxation, and also how to look after my head of hair. He used a hot steam flannel every morning and could ease pressure and headaches in moments by skilful manipulations of the scalp. He was quite a survivor, having known Lord Louis in the days when he was Viceroy of India, long before my time, and he worshipped the ground he stood on, as did all of the surviving footmen and indeed the entire staff at the palace.

It was an experience in itself just to arrive at the presidential palace in Delhi. The central dome was reminiscent of St Paul's. There was colonnade upon colonnade, and you could drive double-decker buses for miles through the passageways. Lord Louis told me that in his time they had 700 servants working in the beautiful sunken gardens alone; 7,000 people living in the compound, including their families, with their own schools, their own society. After the British Raj pulled out, the workforce diminished to some 2,000, and the gardens lost some of their magnificence. But they still kept up standards within the palace. We would be escorted in by the mounted presidential escorts and all the way along the huge colonnades would be an armed soldier every ten feet or so and a *khidmutgar* in a turban, long pantaloons and a white frockcoat with the red presidential crest on it. As we passed along, each footman put his hands together in an Indian gesture of deference and bowed and the soldiers stood to attention. Delhi is one of the few places in the world, possibly the only one remaining, where the old Raj ceremonies are still adhered to in all their impressive formality. The throne-room or 'Durbar' Hall was truly awe-inspiring. When the vast double-doors were opened, they were in direct line with the Triumphant Mall, which led straight into the heart of the city.

Our saddest visit to Delhi was for dear Nehru's funeral in 1964. On this occasion I found myself landed with an almost impossible task. It was May 1964 and Lord Louis was just off to Sandringham while I was in the middle of preparations for yet another tour. He wanted me to accompany him to Norfolk, but I just couldn't cope. There was so much to prepare.

'Look,' I said, 'you're going to Sandringham for two nights. You're returning on Sunday, and we are off on our tour on Sunday afternoon. I really am much too far behind even to consider it. The footman will look after you. I'll fix it with Joe Pearce, the Duke's valet.'

He did not like it – it was one of the very few times I did not accompany him – but grudgingly agreed.

On the Saturday evening I was frantically packing when the telephone rang. It was Lord Louis from Sandringham.

'We've got to go and bury Nehru. You know what we need. See you at Heathrow, eleven a.m. tomorrow.'

And that was it. In the last stages of the tour preparations I had to root out the full ceremonial white tropical uniform with the black mourning armlet and everything else. Then I had to belt up to Heathrow where we had to receive our typhoid, yellow fever and cholera jabs from the doctors in the VIP lounge while our passports were getting the once-over. George Brown was sent with us to represent the Government and Lord Home the Opposition. Since we were representing the Queen, we had a special charter aircraft, and Andy Devine, top correspondent of the *Sunday Times*, and one or two other journalists took passage with us, as did Vice-Admiral Sir Ronald Brockman, the private secretary who had been with Lord Louis since his viceregal days.

Lord Home behaved impeccably on the flight, of course, but the same could not be said for George Brown, the Foreign Secretary. As we prepared for touchdown, Lord Louis got into his ceremonial whites and Lord Home was immaculate in his morning dress. But George Brown was in a soiled and crumpled beige linen suit with a white shirt, open at the neck, and a loose red tie. He had been sleeping fitfully most of the flight and had to be woken up. But he had not washed and looked, I'm afraid, not a pretty sight. Lord Louis told him off in front of all of us. It was a crisis because the heads of governments and assorted VIPs were lined up on the tarmac ready to receive us, with guards of honour and bands, and a special dais for the formal arrival ceremonies, which only colonial India could provide in such style.

'Keep him back, keep him back,' snapped Lord Louis as poor old Mr Brown tried to wander off our aircraft like a tourist.

But that was easier said than done. George Brown pushed his way to the front where Lord Louis blocked his way and said: 'Look, I represent the Queen, so I come first, then you follow me, representing Her Majesty's Government.'

As George Brown reluctantly gave way, Lord Louis glanced at me and said: 'Do not let him be seen until the formal guard inspection is over.'

Fortunately, George Brown was too bleary-eyed to see through the paltry pretext we had invented. I offered to help him to tidy up and so face was saved. But it had taken all our tact and diplomacy to sidetrack him until at least the National Anthem had been played. Lord Louis was more than usually angry at the thought of Her Majesty's representative at the funeral of such a great statesman being seen worldwide in such a state.

When we got to the palace, everything was in chaos, and it was Lord Louis who took charge. The organisers had allowed an hour and a half for the cortège to reach the site for the cremation. Lord Louis, remembering Gandhi's funeral, said that it was going to take more than three times as long to get through the milling crowds, and so it proved. We were in the President's huge black Buick, which was being lifted almost bodily into the air as the crowds shouted: 'Long live Mountbatten! Long live Mountbatten!' We had no choice but to keep the windows closed, even though the temperature must have risen to 120 degrees. I sat in the front as the sweat poured off my peaked cap and dripped down my nose while the car rocked with the adulation of millions of friendly Indians.

When at last we reached the banks of the Ganges, I found it a terrible sight to see dear Nehru lying in an open coffin, high on a raised funeral pyre with scented sandalwood being heaped all around him, to have to watch while he was set alight, to listen to the chanting. I can see him now standing at the window at Broadlands staring out at the beautiful gardens, the rose bud which I had brought him in his buttonhole. I prefer to remember the great man like that.

Within the year, we were back in Delhi for the funeral of Shri Lal Bahadur Shastri, who had succeeded Nehru as Prime Minister. Once again the funeral was held on the banks of the Ganges. I have never experienced such a mass of humanity anywhere in the world; I doubt whether there have ever been so many people in one place as at the funerals of these three Indian leaders, Gandhi, Nehru and Shastri.

On the subject of funerals, Lord Louis, as Chief of the Defence Staffs, had been responsible for the arrangements for Churchill's funeral, code-named Operation Hope-Not, in 1965. Churchill had requested 'lots of military bands', which created something of a problem, as lots of bands and troops are not likely to be readily available without much forward planning. As Churchill went into a coma Lord Louis discussed the problem with Sir John Colville, Churchill's private secretary.

'Don't worry, Dickie,' said Colville, 'he won't die quite yet. Not until 24 January.'

'How can you possibly know that?' asked Lord Louis.

'Because he always said he would die on the day of his father's death, and I am certain he will do just that.'

Lord Louis took a gamble and organised the state funeral for the end of January. Churchill did not let him down. He died not only on the day, but almost on the hour of his father's passing, and consequently the state funeral was a great ceremony and went off without a hitch – the old hero would have been very happy with it. Certainly a case of mind over matter.

The two men had a long-standing friendship. As a young midshipman cadet at the Royal Naval College on the Isle of

Wight, Prince Louis (as he then was) had been spokesman for the cadets when Churchill, as First Lord of the Admiralty, paid a visit. It was a Sunday and the cadets were at supper.

'Well, Dickie, how are you?' asked the great man.

'Very well, sir.'

'Any problems? Anything I can do for you?'

'Just one thing, sir. Would it be possible for us to have *two* sardines for supper on Sunday instead of just the one as we get very hungry?'

'Most certainly,' said Churchill and, turning to the accompanying officers, said: 'See that these young gentlemen get extra sardines for supper.'

But Lord Louis had heard from his mother that Churchill was unreliable. Churchill had borrowed a favourite book from her and broken his promise to return it. After this she always categorised him as 'that most unreliable man'. Lord Louis was not inclined to revise this opinion as the weeks passed and the second sardine never appeared. He made a mental note: Winston Churchill – most unreliable.

When Churchill offered Lord Louis the Supreme Allied Command of South-east Asia in 1943, at the height of the war, Lord Louis asked for time to think it over. Churchill asked immediately what more could he hope for in this war than to be sunk in a bigger and more expensive ship! At that, Lord Mountbatten made up his mind to accept the post.

Three years later, when he actually was Supreme Allied Commander South-east Asia, he was recalled by Churchill, Prime Minister of the Coalition. At Number Ten, Churchill ushered him into his private study, moved to the windows and looked both ways, checked the door and returned to whisper into Lord Louis' ear: 'We're going to drop the bomb.' This was a reference to the Hiroshima atom bomb, a most secret weapon. 'Tell your Chiefs of Staff to prepare to receive the surrender of the Japanese forces in ten days' time.'

Lord Louis was even more stunned when it became clear that it was Churchill's intention that *no one* was to be told how this surrender was to be achieved, not the C-in-Cs, not his own staff, not anyone.

'How could I possibly go back and tell my Area C-in-Cs this? They would tell me I should be locked away and relieved of the Supreme Command.' But this is what he had to do. He gathered his staff and told them to be prepared for the surrender, and, as he had anticipated, most of them assumed that their Supreme Commander had 'gone over the top'.

I became familiar down the years with these and numerous other Churchill stories from Lord Louis' speeches in which he often included them, and the long car journeys on which we rehearsed those speeches together.

Ethiopia in 1965 was a special one-off trip as part of the farewell to the world tour, for which we were guests of the Emperor Haile Selassie, who was of course later assassinated. We drove through Addis Ababa in the Emperor's limousine and the whole city went on its knees as we passed. At the palace, which I thought ostentatious, at the top of the steps, on stout gold chains, were some wicked-looking leopards which growled as we walked past them. I wondered why, when he was renowned as the Lion of Judah, the Emperor had leopards on guard at his front door. Whatever the reason, they terrified the life out of me!

A picnic was organised for us in the mountains where the air was cooler. I remember seeing leaving the palace a convoy of asses, mouldy-looking and half-starved creatures, and on their poor backs in palliasses rolls of carpet, tents, armchairs, wicker baskets and heaven knows what.

Lady Patricia, who was Lord Louis' official hostess for the trip, asked me: 'What do you think all those are for?'

'I can't imagine,' I said, 'unless he is moving house.'

The answer to the puzzle was provided for us later. The picnic took place in a huge tent which was carpeted on the walls as well as on the floors, with hanging tapestries and chandeliers. The trouble they took for just a picnic!

The Emperor was present, and I spent most of the time filming, relieved that I could avoid eating the food, which appeared to consist of sheep's eyes and other dishes even more alarming to contemplate. And then, of course, all the paraphernalia had to be lugged back down a very craggy, rough path; I felt so sorry for the underfed beasts of burden. So much ostentation in a country so bedevilled by starvation; the contrast was more cynically apparent in Ethiopia than in any other country I visited. Except perhaps in one African country where a huge presidential palace was built with pure crystal chandeliers from Cartier, royal-red, best-quality Wilton carpets with a two-inch pile everywhere you walked, gold-plated bathroom fittings, gilt mirrors and precious metals galore. But outside the gates of the palace mud hovels for the people and starvation for their children. No wonder these self-made gods came to grief; they deserved to.

When I first visited India I had no idea of poverty. I had read about the poor in Calcutta and Bombay, and I knew about the wonderful work Lady Louis was doing for the Save the Children Fund, but it was no preparation for what I was to see at first hand. As we drove through the streets of Delhi I could not believe the crowds, and said to the police commissioner accompanying us: 'Is there something going on? Is the President driving past? Is there a state visit or what?'

'No. Why do you ask?'

'Well, who are all these people on the streets waiting for?'

'They are always on the streets. That is where they live. You see that group of people? They have a tin can and a little pot and that is their home, that is their lot.'

Once, we were guests of the Shah of Persia, another god-like figure who lived in a city inhabited by the poorest of the poor. One evening we were taken into Teheran deep down into the depths of a bank vault where there was a huge concrete bunker. In the bunker was a marble hall the size of a cinema auditorium, and in this marble hall were the Persian Crown Jewels. They were in show cases, created for the Shah by Boucheron of Paris, and each case was teeming with sapphires, diamonds and rubies. There were beehive crowns, tiaras, brooches and necklaces in profusion. It was an Aladdin's cave, and there must have been enough there to feed all the country's poor, yet it was stuck away in the depths of this vault. I cannot guess what instinct it is that drives these shahs and emperors to amass such wealth and to hide it away when outside their palace gates the entire countryside is littered with people dying and starving, children without hope, without homes, without even a glass of water or a piece of bread. How could these potentates sleep in their gold-plated beds at night?

It is no coincidence that both the Shah and Haile Selassie were overthrown, along with Idi Amin of Uganda. Bokassa of the Central African Republic was another dictator who reckoned that there was nobody in the world sufficiently grand to put the crown on his head at his coronation – so he crowned himself. He came to a dismal end too, and, in my opinion, rightly so.

Lord Louis was a 'Gold Card' member of the International Variety Club, which does so much for underprivileged children throughout the world, and in this capacity he undertook a demanding ten-day tour of American cities in 1965. This involved numerous charity dinners, at which people would pay large sums to have dinner in the company of Mountbatten, and Lord Louis would give the principal after-dinner speech. During the mornings and afternoons we would visit hospitals etc., where the latest research was being carried out. The most memorable was the hospital at Minnesota/Minneapolis/St Pauls, where early experiments in open heart surgery were taking place. We were given a whirlwind tour, including a panorama of pigs' livers in clinical glass jars, before being capped and gowned for a visit to the operating theatre. Here a poor old dear was having probes inserted into her heart. One by one our party was reduced until just a handful of us was left. I watched with interest until the pictures appeared in close-up on a television screen, whereupon, feeling the skin on my forehead tightening ominously, I made a quick exit, followed almost at once by Lord Louis, the last to give in!

After this, we were shown what must be one of the saddest sights in the world, a ward of 'cabbage' children, babies born with no hope of consciousness but kept alive in the name of medical research. The doctors were boasting of their skill in keeping so many of these babies alive when Lord Louis simply asked: 'Why? For what kind of future?'

The question seemed to stun them and we were all deep in thought as we left this magnificent world centre for medical research.

The General Mills Corporation of America kindly laid on their company's executive jet for us, and took us around a soya bean production plant. Soya, they told us, could be grown in any of the Third World countries, and could be turned into any variety of nutritious food.

Assembling for a buffet lunch in their offices, we were given cold drinks and crisps. The crisps were delicious and I said as much. Yes, they said, they are soya.

'Don't talk silly,' I said. 'I know a crisp when I see a crisp, and this isn't soya, this is a crisp. It's also the best crisp I've ever tasted.'

'Yes,' they said, 'that's soya bean.'

They took me, still a Doubting Thomas, through to the laboratories, broke open the crisp, and showed me under the microscope the unmistakable strands of the soya bean. It was hard to argue with this evidence. Then we had lunch. Mashed beef roll – what the Americans call hash beef – the meat, the pastry, the gravy, the potatoes, all soya. Everything we ate was soya, and it was delicious. I would not have believed it if I had not seen it under the microscope. I still marvel at such ingenuity.

As part of their research programme they had picked up a boy of about ten from one of the poorest tribes in Africa, a typical case of malnutrition with a potbelly and sores. They showed us a lifesize photograph of him as he had been, and then they showed us another photograph of him six months later, healthy, trim, fit, a lovely-looking boy. They told us about the difficulties they had had getting him to eat at all. They put him on an intensive soya diet with soya chicken, soya bacon, soya sausage, soya everything they could think of. He would touch none of it; he would not even look at it. Until at length the scientists came up with the idea that his native food was rotting fish. This was their biggest challenge. They could produce all these flavours, every flavour known to modern gourmets, but there was no way they could produce rotting, stinking fish. Until at last they succeeded and the boy made what could only be described as a miraculous recovery.

What gratitude we owe to these brilliant dedicated people, doctors and scientists, who devote their lives to finding new ways of feeding the starving millions and how sad that all their research seems to have done so little to relieve the terrible situation of the poor peoples in the Third World.

Lord Louis travelled extensively in his role as Chief of the UK Defence Staff, while also heading the Commonwealth Independence and Immigration Commissions. He was a serviceman and a civilian and a royal. And wherever he went I went with him, whether it was to the military front lines, a Government House, a swish hotel, an embassy, a royal palace or whatever.

Our constant globe-trotting on military and public duty took us to many strange lands and brought us face to face with many of what ignorant people used to call the 'uncivilised' tribes, the proud Ashantis in Africa, the natives living in tiny mud huts by the shores of Lake Rudolf in what is now Zimbabwe, the magnificent ebony black horsemen of Kano in the deserts of northern Nigeria with their brilliantly coloured robes, the Incas in their llama wool shawls and bowler hats, the flower-bedecked Polynesian lads and lasses. We were lucky. We saw these splendid sights and met these splendid people before the tourist 'rape' began, and for this I am eternally grateful.

Within twenty years, Tahiti and Fiji, once the islands of tropical dreams, have become concrete jungles and nuclear testing fields. As the places change, so do the people. I find it sad that so much natural beauty and so many peaceful peoples should be made the same in the name of progress.

Grass skirts and floral leis are replaced by plastic ones, made in Taiwan. Those paradise islands are landscaped with tower-blocks. The Japanese have invaded the business world there, and endless huge liners disgorge thousands of peroxided American lady tourists.

Modern jets and package holidays have diminished our world. While it is proper that everyone should have the opportunity to investigate our planet, it is tragic that so much has had to be forfeited to enable this to come about, even to the point of extinction for so many once noble and proud tribes, their customs and their environment. It is a heavy price to pay.

Lord Louis would have been very sad to see the destruction of the rain forests which has happened since he died. The climatic changes will no doubt affect us all in time – and not for the better. Lord Louis did his utmost to warn government ministers around the globe of the problems facing the world from the destruction of the environment and the population explosion, but his advice fell on deaf ears in many quarters. Travelling as much as he did gave him (and me) a great insight into the problems of mankind which would be of unfathomable use today.

Chapter Nine
A Blue Lobster

Classiebawn Castle in County Sligo is a mock-Gothic mini-castle on the shores of the Bay of Donegal. It was inherited along with an estate of 10,000 acres by the first Lord Palmerston. As a child, Lady Louis had spent her Augusts there, and the tradition was continued after her death. Lord Louis rented it to private parties for the rest of the year, so that the staff who looked after us in August could remain in permanent employment and Classiebawn could be self-supporting.

They were a lovely lot of people, local Irish girls and boys, and I was particularly fond of Peter, who was training to be the butler. He was very young and soft-spoken, polite, friendly, nothing too much trouble. One time we took him to Broadlands with us to learn the ropes. He was not at all fussed, and even when the Queen visited us he took it very much in his stride. The only thing was he would keep saying: 'Aye, OK.'

Lord Louis asked me to see if I could not get him to break this irritating habit.

'Look, Peter,' I said, 'we don't go round saying "Aye, OK" all the time. Would you just say "Thank you" or "Yes, m'lord" in future and leave it at that?'

'Aye, OK,' said Peter.

I had to give up.

The family solicitors in Sligo were actually called Argue and Phibbs. Can you believe that!

Classiebawn Castle looks foreboding, perched on a rocky

peninsula with the sea on three sides. Across the bay are the beautiful blue mountains of Donegal and behind the house rise the mountains of Sligo and Ben Bulben, underneath which is buried the poet W. B. Yeats.

> Cast a cold eye
> On life and death
> Horseman, ride by

is the epitaph carved on the modest headstone. To the south on a clear day you can just make out the mountains of Mayo, and Achille Island on a super-clear day.

The castle itself always used to put me in mind of Wuthering Heights, but appearances are deceptive. Indoors it was warm, loving and cosy. It had none of the antiques and luxuries of Broadlands; it was by no means a palace; it was a comfortable holiday home and an ideal haven on that rugged and sometimes hostile coast.

Besides Lord Louis, his two daughters and their families also spent August at Classiebawn. Lady Patricia and her husband, Lord Brabourne, arrived with a nanny to keep their seven children in order – at the age of forty Lady Patricia had surprised everyone by giving birth to twins, Nicholas and Timothy. Lady Pamela and David Hicks brought their three young children. Princess Alice, Lord Louis' sister and Prince Philip's mother, was always determined to come, and Crown Prince Gustav of Sweden joined us once in his mid-teens. There might be an occasional granny or a family friend as well, but the party was never too large or too formal. The political situation discouraged the principal members of the Royal Family from coming, but they were accustomed in any case to spend their holidays at Balmoral and Sandringham.

One year there was an entirely false rumour in the press that Princess Margaret was coming to visit us. The roads down to the jetty were blocked for miles with sightseers and the press refused to leave us alone. One day, the family decided on a shopping expedition to Sligo. Lord Brabourne and Lord Louis were in one car when they became aware of another car following them at high speed. Lord Brabourne assumed that they must be journalists and determined to try and shake them off. At which point a Keystone-Cops-style chase through the back streets of Sligo got under way, until finally the two lords found themselves in a dead end. Emerging from the car, Lord Brabourne blasted at them: 'You bloody press, why can't you ever just leave us alone to go shopping?' Only to be told that the 'pressmen' were their Special Branch police escorts trying to keep up with them.

Most summers, Lord Brabourne would spend ten days or so in County Mayo, trout- and salmon-fishing. I would drive him down, stay overnight, and return to Classiebawn.

Once settled in, our days would be spent in and around *Shadow V*, the lovely old boat, the fifth of that name, built with wood from the estate, and which the locals always referred to as *Shadow Vee*. Lord Louis had her painted green and white, the same colours as the admirals' barges (or 'Green Parrots') in the Royal Navy, and fitted her out with two-way radio communication with the castle (which he was obliged to have at all times), a shark-fishing swivel chair, a small cabin, a loo and a little phut-phut Perkins marine diesel engine. The press liked to characterise her as a magnificently appointed and luxurious yacht or converted trawler, but she was just an old lobster-pot and shark-fishing boat, on which we spent hundreds of happy hours as well as some very anxious moments.

These would often occur when Lord Louis put one of the very youngest of the grandchildren on the wheel and another on the gear-handle as we endeavoured to manoeuvre out of harbour. The great man would be sitting in the shark-fishing chair shouting out: 'Ahead! Stop Engines! Astern! Astern!' while the girls cried at me: 'Which way is that, CPO Evans?' Holidaymakers on the jetty giggled, unaware that the old boy in the seaman's sweater and cap was Lord Louis or that the old lady in the mac and headscarf was the Queen of Sweden.

The local fishermen were sceptical about our shark-fishing exploits, insisting that there were no sharks off Donegal in August. They looked at us with greater respect when we landed a bluenose, about 280 lbs of it, which was just a pound or two short of the UK record for that species.

Lobster-potting was an unforgettable experience. The first requirement was to catch mackerel for fresh bait, before setting off round the headland and up to the Black Rocks, where we had our six pots on buoys. We would usually catch enough mackerel for breakfast and for the Rubby Dubby Tin, as well as for lobster bait. (The Rubby Dubby Tin was kept stocked with rotting fish for when we went after sharks.) As we hauled in the pots we would sing 'What Shall We Do with the Drunken Sailor?' but adding our own silly words like 'Put him in the Rubby Dubby Tin till he's sober', and the excitement was intense as we hauled up the pots. Besides lobsters, there would be crabs and the occasional eel.

As well as shark-fishing and lobster-potting, we might fish for pollack, tope, skate and mackerel, which we would smoke and eat immediately. There is absolutely nothing to beat freshly smoked mackerel straight from the sea.

Lord Louis, who had organised armies and sub-continents and parliamentary commissions, found considerable problems with grandchildren. With so many of them all wanting to trail mackerel lines at once, we always ended up in a disastrous tangle. And this was not helped by the probability that one of the tiniest of the children would be at the wheel, so that we zig-zagged all over the bay. Fortunately, we had a king on hand, and it was dear old King Gustav who solved our problem with the gift of a newly designed Swedish Paravane float, ingeniously employing a ball and fin. With six of these floats and by carefully working out the different 'tacks', we could safely and tangle-free troll six lines at varying depths. The result was an enormously increased catch in a fraction of the time. One day we turned up a huge sky-blue lobster, a great rarity, and sent it off to the Zoological Society in London for research.

Even the children's playtime in the sand was studiously organised. Deep channels would be dug in obedience to a grand Mountbatten design of dams and reservoirs. Then, when the tide was on the turn, the channels would fill up with rushing water, creating enormous fun for all. Then there was the systematic prawning at tide's ebb in the harbour at Mullaghmore. Each bunch of seaweed would be thoroughly shuffled by the huge prawn net which Lord Louis had designed – a broad straight forebar and a deep net were the secret. I felt so sad for some tiny little child left holding

Grandpa's prawning bucket and being bawled at to remove the creatures crawling in the slimy bilge brought up in each dredging. Prawns, caught in the net, are almost translucent and look nothing like the pretty pink things served up for tea, so it was difficult for these little people, maybe only six or seven years old, to distinguish them amongst the seaweed and moss, the shells and rock-crabs.

'There's one, grab it, grab it!' Lord Louis would shout. 'Hurry up, come on, hurry up!'

Sometimes I wondered why the prawns had not all scuttled out to sea in terror. The fresh prawns were taken to the castle kitchens where Lord Louis would supervise their preparation. He also took charge of serving them to the family at tea, rationing them out as meticulously as if they were gold dust. By then they would look gloriously pink and succulent.

'One for you, one for me, one for you, one for me,' he would say, and all the grandchildren would be counting carefully to make sure that no one had more than his or her share. They made wonderful eating with huge chunks of brown Irish soda bread.

Other afternoons might find the family galloping the horses along the edge of the surf chased by the dogs, the massive Atlantic rollers curling and breaking along the beautiful sandy beaches. The horses would have to dodge the ribcages of the Armada shipwrecks that still litter parts of that wild coastline. There was no finer activity than this to sharpen the appetite, aided by the fresh spray-filled Atlantic air.

There was never the luxury of a lie-in. It would be breakfast at eight, boat at nine thirty if the weather was kind. Besides fishing and riding, there were shopping expeditions to Sligo or Donegal Town and idyllic picnics on the lovely remote island of Innishmurry some eight miles off the coast. The island offered us a pretty little natural harbour amongst the rocks so that, if the sea was calm, it was possible to sail right ashore. We explored the primitive ruins of a cashel, or settlement, consisting of tiny dome-shaped houses in a small circular cluster, but the only regular inhabitants were the wild rabbits and a few sheep landed in a cradle ferry from the mainland and enjoying the rough grazing. Then there would be fun and games, with treasure hunts and swimming in the icy Atlantic if the weather permitted.

From Innishmurry, Classiebawn looked almost beautiful, high up on huge cliffs, its standard fluttering from the high tower, and against the backcloth of majestic Ben Bulben.

After a tiring day at sea, there were jigsaw puzzles in the evening. The family had joined the Jigsaw Club, and every couple of days or so new 2,000-piece puzzles would arrive in special boxes for everyone to pore over. Or, too exhausted by their exertions even for jigsaws, some would read or doze. I seldom remember seeing himself reading a book normally, but these were amongst the few occasions when he did. His choice was a little improbable: usually Perry Mason thrillers in French or German to give him a chance to brush up on his languages. There was a late tea for the children in the nursery, followed by family dinner, for which there might be an occasional guest, local friends such as the Duke of Westminster and his son Gerald, now the present Duke, or Derek Hill, the artist.

Family conferences were held to deal with domestic problems. These would range from what furnishings were due for renovations, or reupholstery, to what repairs *Shadow V* needed. Occasionally a major issue would be raised, a new waterpump perhaps, and then Rodney, the local boatbuilder, was called in.

These holidays were my holidays too. My life was so involved with Lord Louis' that I found it easier to be constantly 'on the job' than to try to relax, or go elsewhere only to be recalled within twenty-four hours for some drama or other. Once you are geared up to such a high pitch of activity, it is actually quite painful to try to unwind properly. Besides all this, I loved the west coast of Ireland!

However, it was most unusual for us to escape our official duties for long. One year, I was closing down Wilton Crescent and packing for Classiebawn when I learnt that Lord Louis was to present new standards to the British Legion in Belfast before driving to the west coast. We never travelled anywhere without fulfilling engagements en route. Then came another request: Princess Alexandra was to have taken the passing-out Sovereign's Parade at Sandhurst, but she had developed tonsillitis, so could we please try to fit that in as well? No problem. Until another message arrived that the Queen

Mother had gone down with a flu bug and was not going to be able to present standards that afternoon to a new regiment based at Munchengladbach in West Germany. Well, all right, we can do that too.

After much shuffling of arrangements we drove down that morning to Sandhurst, represented Her Majesty, inspected the parade, addressed the military cadets who were passing out as officers into the Army, cut out the formal lunch which followed the parade, changed in the car as we speeded off to a small air-strip in Hampshire where a fast R A F plane was awaiting us. We grabbed a bite of lunch as we flew on to Munchengladbach, transferring into a helicopter which landed at the back of the officers' mess, the parade all ready and waiting. Changing in the general's quarters, Lord Louis donned full ceremonial dress for the second time. (I had given it a quick clean in the aircraft.) After the presentation of standards, inspection of the parade, the march-past and the big speech, we mingled with the families and performed the necessary courtesies. Then it was back into the chopper, back into the aircraft, a cup of welcome R A F tea, and north to Belfast, where they had put back their ceremony until the evening. By eight o'clock we were with the British Legion in Belfast, and there we stayed for two hours.

Leaving Belfast at ten p.m., we arrived at Classiebawn in the early hours, somewhat exhausted, after having covered so many miles and been on the move for so long.

This was exceptional, because official functions as they affect the Royal Family are meticulously organised, in Lord Louis' case probably eighteen months or two years in advance. The Court closes down for August and September when the Royal Family move to Balmoral, and during these months official engagements are kept to a strict minimum. But there always has to be somebody on duty. Illness and death do not always fit into programmes or Royal Diaries.

Even at Classiebawn Lord Louis was unable to wind down. Once, as I was preparing for the holiday, he asked me: 'Make sure we've got plenty of extra foolscap.'

I did not expect this, which was pretty unusual, as I normally knew or could anticipate what was in the wind. A little puzzled, I did as he said.

The mystery was resolved when I found him working late into the nights, organising the unification of the three defence services, as Macmillan had requested. In longhand he set out the future unified policy for the Royal Navy, the Army and the Air Force, and took great trouble with it, because it was something he passionately cared about. It was no easy task. There were very senior officers in each of the services who were hidebound by tradition, and limited by their own historical pig-headedness. When the move to the new Ministry of Defence was being undertaken, there were First Lords of the Admiralty who had been in situ since the Admiralty was formed, there were generals from the War Office for whom the status quo was hallowed, and the Royal Air Force hierarchy who prided themselves on their independence. Only Lord Louis could have managed to get them all to move, happily enough in the end, to adjoining offices in the new and central Ministry of Defence, where the Chiefs of Staff could meet with the minimum of fuss, and could, while retaining a measure of independence, co-ordinate in a successfully unified command structure, not unlike a mini-Pentagon.

Another August Lord Louis devoted himself to writing an historical account of Innishmurry and its ancient settlement. This was intended as a guide for the Americans who would be renting Classiebawn. Characteristically, he wanted them to be able to get as much pleasure from Classiebawn as possible and took enormous trouble over this, the only known history of the place. He was helped, of course, by several professors of history in Dublin, and talked to many of the locals.

My last summer at Classiebawn was as hectic as ever. For three years (1965–1968) London Weekend Television had been working with Lord Louis on a twelve-part television series, *The Life and Times of Lord Mountbatten*, and this had involved all of us in a great deal of extra effort – me especially. There had been visits to those parts of the world most closely connected with Lord Louis' career, endless scripts for him to study, and there had been the additional pressure involved in having the team of the producer, Peter Morley, and the writer and the historian, John Terraine, living with us for such an extended time. It was suddenly too much for me.

Although our Augusts in Classiebawn had been intended as my holidays as well as holidays for the family, I don't think I ever really relaxed. I suppose I had got out of the habit. For ten years I had rarely had one day entirely free of responsibility. I had shared Lord Louis' life. I had done all the wonderful things he had done, met the great people, visited the most beautiful places, seen the most remarkable sights, and worked solidly all the hours which God gave. For ten years I had lived in his shadow. I could almost think for him. Let me amend that: I *did* think for him. He never had to tell me what he needed. I knew before he asked, and could always correctly anticipate the answer he would give and whatever he needed – with the one exception of pink pyjamas for snorkelling!

I had no other life. When you live with someone so great and so dynamic, you become wholly attached, fixated, mentally and physically. You become one unit. And so, if he never eased up – and he never did – no more could I. I find it easy to forgive him, if forgiveness is in order.

Of course, he too had been under enormous pressure. He was reorganising the defence strategy, he was touring the world on independence and immigration commissions, he was investigating the prisons, he was involved in some 280 organisations and was never content to be merely a figurehead. Neither of us had a chance of a private life, and he relied on me totally to have everything in the right place at the right time.

So what if occasionally I muttered under my breath: 'I don't know how you expect me to cope with all this.'

He would mutter back: 'It must be because of your great ability and your natural charm – that, after all, is why you were picked for the job.'

At which point he would glance at me and we would both burst out laughing. Maybe such moments had helped to keep us both sane. To be fair, he had always insisted: 'Tell me if anything is too much or if you can't cope.'

But of course I never did. Perhaps it would have been better if I had, though I was never one for bleating. He went off on his family picnics, but I was always packing up, loading up, supervising the households, working out the next port of call, making sure we had plenty of this and were not going to run out of that. I had many of the problems. Later on, I was told that he had written in his dairy: 'Evans showing signs of a breakdown.'

Few on his staff escaped strain and few lasted very long. I had been warned for years that I, too, would collapse sooner or later. I guess my time had arrived.

I must assume that he had noticed something. Had I been short-tempered? They always say that you never notice these signs yourself. But whatever he had observed he never insisted on my taking a break. Once you showed any signs of failing, he would assume that you might fail again. He would do what he could for you, but you were no longer one hundred per cent and that was little use to him. He always said – and stated it publicly in the television series – that he hated sacking people, but that it was fatal to keep somebody in a job when they were clearly no longer up to it. He was talking about commanding officers at the time, and it is obviously wrong to put many lives at risk because of incompetence at the top.

We were at Classiebawn. There was a misunderstanding, which I will not write about. I was so close to the edge that the least little incident would have pushed me over. It was Saturday. Lord Louis, just in from the sea, was downstairs and he asked me to get him a folder from the despatch box in his room. I did so. On top of the despatch box was a report from the Broadlands private secretary and the name Evans on a sheet of paper caught my eye, though I never read any papers. Curiosity proved too strong for me. I read a sentence: 'Evans is very ill. We knew this when he left the Service.' I could not read any more. If I had, I would have known that the letter was not referring to me at all and that my name had been confused with the name of somebody else on his staff. But I did not. I only found this out much later.

I took the foolscap down to him, and said nothing. If I had mentioned it he would have known that I had looked at his private papers. I doubt whether I would have mentioned it in any case. All the time the anxiety was tightening inside me. I was becoming almost paranoid and felt so ill that I was convinced that I was dying from some incurable disease.

The next morning I felt that I could not continue any longer. I had to leave. By chance, it was the only time that I had had my little Triumph Spitfire sports car with me at Classiebawn. I loaded my few personal belongings into it and drove off, saying nothing to anyone.

I kept my foot down all the way to Belfast. My mind was so confused that it never occurred to me that there would be no Liverpool ferries sailing on a Sunday. It had been in my mind to get the Liverpool ferry, but where to? Broadlands? I felt that I could not go back there. I just wanted to be alone. When I found that there were no sailings to Liverpool it threw me entirely. They said to me at the docks: 'You'll get a ferry at Larne for Stranraer.' And I thought: Yes. That will do. Larne is only a half an hour's drive from Belfast. I'll go and have a few quiet days in Scotland.

But the minute I got to Larne docks I was surrounded by police. A charming inspector asked me: 'Are you Chief Petty Officer Evans? [Though I had actually left the Navy in 1965, my old title still stuck] We've had a message from Classiebawn. Lord Mountbatten wants you to ring him before you leave.' He added that he would see that the ferry waited for me while I made the call. His instructions had been to hold me until I had spoken to Lord Mountbatten.

For fifteen minutes we tried, but could not get through. The Irish telephone system in those days was still on the crank handle. The ferry captain was growing increasingly annoyed at the delay, and finally I said: 'I'm sorry, but I must get on this boat,' to which the inspector reluctantly replied: 'Well, I have no authority to hold you.' To reassure him, I promised to ring Lord Louis from the other side of the Irish Sea. But I had no intention of doing so. I was allowed to board.

I landed at Stranraer and drove off into the middle of nowhere. I drove northwards, although there was no logic to that. Everyone and everything I knew was to the south. I had plenty of friends, but people who have lived through what I was then living through will understand that friends are the last people you want to be with at such a time. Friends and family are there to rally round, but friends and family are the last people you want. You prefer to make a clean break. I did. Days passed in oblivion.

I was sitting by a loch getting deeper and deeper into

depression and despair, wondering about the illness I imagined they were shielding me from, with a load of pills and the intention of ending it all, when I heard on the car radio, which was often on, the news of the death of Princess Marina, the Duchess of Kent. Instinctively the royal part of my mind went into automatic action. I believe this news flash saved my life.

Oh my God, I thought. They will all be coming back. I pointed the car southwards and started driving. I drove all night and all the following day towards Hampshire. There were no motorways in those days and it was a very hard slog. My depression deepened rather than eased. In Swindon I was stopped by a motorcycle; it was a policeman, who had me up for speeding. I explained that I was on Lord Mountbatten's staff, that I had just heard the news about Princess Marina, and that I was hurrying to Broadlands. He dropped all charges and escorted me out of Swindon, making sure that I was on the right road. That policeman was the first person I had spoken to for days.

I knew what I would find and I found it. The family would be returning from Ireland just a week into their holiday and Charles would be in a flap. Indeed, he hardly knew what to say or do. The brouhaha and panic was just what I needed. I went back to work.

When Lord Louis arrived, he merely said: 'Are you all right?' I think that he hoped that, since I had given no formal notice, whatever it was that had been troubling me would melt away. It did not. I gave in my resignation and it was accepted in his handwritten reply. Lord Louis told me that he had asked his private secretary, Commander Webb, to try to help me sort out my affairs in as sympathetic a way as possible. (This was a reference to any debts I might owe the estate for the rebuilding and refurbishment of the converted mews flat I had worked so long and hard on.) I had asked for a three months' 'work-out' in which to train up a replacement and to tie up any loose ends. He agreed at once. But as each day dawned, my poor old heart grew heavier and heavier, for I was leaving the life I loved, the house I loved and the people I loved so much. They were my only family. But I also knew that there could be no turning back.

*   *   *

Lord Mountbatten was leaving for the USA, and completing his dressing for the trip. I was still carrying on the best I could, but now of course things were very different. For the first time, I was not going with him and that felt extremely strange. But I coped with everything and was profoundly grateful that I was so busy. His secretary would be standing in as valet for this trip, which was only a short one. I had loaded the luggage and explained as best I could to the secretary Lord Louis' routines and requirements. Fortunately, as this was not a complicated military trip, no uniforms would be required.

The time had come to say goodbye. I held out the jacket of his suit for him to put on; neither of us could speak much, and we both had tears in our eyes. Then he took my hand and firmly shook it. It seemed very strange. It was a thing we had never done since saying hello all those years before. He put a hand on my shoulder, his most endearing gesture of great affection, and said: 'Well, cheerio, old son, look after yourself.' And he was gone, flying down the stairs, into the car, and away.

It was then that the final blow hit me. I knew that by the time he returned in a few days' time, I would be sailing across the Atlantic to a new life.

I had never felt ill. In fact I had never for one moment seriously thought about my own health. In the Royal Navy we had a thorough medical, including X-rays, every twelve months, and, as far as I knew, I was in first-class condition, though of course lately I had been so anxious to discover what was really wrong with me. My poor old mind was in turmoil with this 'mystery illness'. I had felt well enough though, apart from that burnt-out feeling in my poor old brainbox, but I had come close to convincing myself that, whatever it might be, my future really didn't matter any more. I was just thirty-seven years old.

My new life was to be on the island of Mustique in my beloved Caribbean. I had my entire possessions with me, such as they were, having given virtually everything I owned away, and I had decided to sail rather than fly, to give myself a much needed break for ten days or so. My passage was booked on board the French liner *Antilles*. Since she had commenced her outward journey from Le Havre, she was not actually berthing in Southampton. So it was on a drizzly Saturday evening in November that I was driven away from Broadlands. I was glad it was a Saturday, which meant that there would be fewer people around, and I was glad it was dark so early. My dear old friend, Ron Heath, the maintenance manager, drove me off to Southampton docks, where I boarded the tugboat tender to join the *Antilles*. She looked so romantic, all twinkling lights, and typical French matelots were on hand to receive me with my luggage. Since there was a fair breeze blowing, it was quite a tricky and dramatic move to get the dozen or so passengers safely on board.

We sailed at once, and I went on deck to watch England and her shore lights fading away into the darkness. By now it was eleven o'clock and I was suddenly devastatingly tired. I could not face the late dinner provided for us and turned in in my little cabin, surrounded by my entire belongings, without the heart to unpack anything other than my toothbrush. It was then that I cried myself into a fitful sleep. I had never felt so low in my life; yet I could not muster the energy to care. I felt that I had nothing to live for, and maybe not even long to live, even though I was going to such a beautiful island, to my beloved West Indies, and to my destiny, whatever it might be.

I had left my heart, my soul, and all that I loved at Broadlands, which had been so much a part of my life. I had scarcely ever thought of life beyond it and now, as I found myself in this alien situation, I was almost numbed by the feeling of a lack of purpose in my existence. So I lay in my cabin, endlessly trying to think of what had happened to put me in this hopeless pickle. What had I done wrong? But I could find no answers, and perhaps there were none. Perhaps I shall never know the reason why. I only know that I felt completely physically and mentally burnt out. Nothing mattered any more. I was finished. Mountbattenitis had struck me its final blow.

Chapter Ten
Mullaghmore Revisited

In the following ten years Lord Louis and I met occasionally, when I was in service with the Duke of Westminster at Ely Island in County Fermanagh, just north of the border from Classiebawn. Every August the Mountbatten family would visit us and spend the day on the Duke's yacht, *Trasna*. Lord Louis was just the same as in the old days.

The last time they arrived at the jetty in August 1979, with various friends, *Trasna* was waiting. There was lunch and tea on board, and everything was prepared for a grand day's sailing. Well, maybe not quite everything.

I knew we would get a rocket, because we were not flying the Union Jack at the mainmast. The Union Jack is traditionally flown to denote that an Admiral of the Fleet is on board, but, as we did not have one small enough, the commander, who was the Duke's cousin, said not to worry. I knew better. To make amends, I dashed back to the house just before the Mountbatten party arrived and got my tape machine and a tape I had of Royal Marine marches, which included 'Rule Britannia'. 'Rule Britannia' happens to be the musical salute – that is to say, eight bars of it are – to an Admiral of the Fleet.

Lord Louis arrived at the yacht, and predictably, as soon as he was about to board, noticed the omission and blasted us for not flying the flag, at which point I pressed the button and 'Rule Britannia' blurted out beautifully over the water. This absolutely flattened him and, with a very broad smile, he returned the salute and immediately forgave us. He was so chuffed that I heard him muttering to my duchess: 'Trust Evans to come up with that!'

Our day was off to a great start after all. It was as if I had never left him.

After a day spent cruising the lough, we had tea. I had found a new brand of cake called a Battenberg slice, which tickled Lord Louis pink. I knew at once that he would ask for the wrapper, and I had it ready for him when he did. It seemed strange to me that we were able to pick up at once where we had left off all those years before. It was as though as soon as he appeared I went straight into Mountbatten top gear.

We got back to the jetty, and he left arm in arm with my duchess, heading for his car. Then he shook hands with me, just the same as before, and used the same words: 'Cheerio, old son, look after yourself.'

But it seemed to me that this time there was a deeper sadness in his eyes, as if he knew that it was to be the last time, and so it turned out to be.

Four days later, a few miles down the road, he was brutally murdered.

It took me ten years to gather sufficient courage to go back to the scene of the Mullaghmore tragedy. Until then I had not the heart for it, and could not raise the will, though I felt that one day I must return and lay the ghost of the bitterness and sadness which has filled my heart ever since that awful day.

Outside the tourist season, the whole place was deserted. It was a clear, chilly day. I went down the coast road, past the bleak-looking remote castle which had once been full of the sound of giggling, happy children. Now I could hear only the crashing of the wild sea on the black rocks below, that familiar stretch of the Atlantic which, in happier times, had borne dear old *Shadow V* so safely to Innishmurry and to the lobster-pots. Then her valuable cargo had been future kings and queens and princes; now she and her cargo were shattered and bits of her soul were still being tossed around on that very same seabed along with parts of the bodies of those who had been so precious to me.

I stood on that cold cliff, overlooking the scene of the explosion, and the tears welled up into my eyes. I was back on

Shadow, hauling up those pots with those happy young boys as we cleared the decks for action. I could see it all so vividly from my sad vantage point: those years of happiness, those wonderful people, wiped out in one foul, violent and senseless, merciless, murderous act, carried out by such misguided, bigoted and grossly ignorant beings – perhaps they can explain it to the Almighty on their day of reckoning, which they will surely have to in time, but I have no doubt that they are damned to darkest hell itself for all eternity.

I was able to visit some of the village people, folks I had known who are now much older and wiser, who are still ashamed and sad about what happened. They are no longer the carefree happy-go-lucky people I had previously known. Was I fully facing up to the past? I sensed a guilt, a very deep guilt.

Stories I was told made me quite sick, stories of local men who had remarked that they would sleep much better at night now that 'the royals had been put away'. What sort of people can they be who think that by violently murdering an old man of almost eighty, a sweet innocent boy of fourteen and another of sixteen, one of their own countrymen, a dear, wonderful old lady and a harmless little dog, they might create a better world in which to live? I cannot begin to understand. The one thing I am sure of is that neither the perpetrators of this wicked murder nor any of those who support them will ever know true peace of mind, and that they will face their Day of Judgement and pay the price. The family so terribly taken away that day are now in Paradise, nestled in the arms of the Almighty, safe from harm, and enjoying their reward in heaven, as befits their time on earth.

When asked whether he feared death, Lord Louis would always answer: 'No, I have no fear of dying, so long as it is peacefully, painlessly and quietly in my sleep. I have done and enjoyed so many things, I could not have wished for a more satisfying and contented life.'

Having served his country for sixty-seven years, and particularly the defence of its peoples, enabling them to enjoy freedom and democracy, I know he was prepared to give his own life for it. I find it so very sad that such a magnificent man who had given so much to the world in the cause of peace should not have been granted a peaceful end. He deserved a more precious route to Paradise.

As I write, March 1989, ten years on, during my return to Mullaghmore, a handsome young British soldier serving his country was, along with another serviceman, violently murdered by the same terrorists. He was twenty-four, and had his whole life ahead of him. He left a loving family and his sweet young fiancée, a pretty nurse, to grieve over him for the rest of their lives. This same soldier had had premonitions that if he was sent to Northern Ireland he might well be killed by the very people he had been sent to protect. So he wrote to his loved ones, quoting a poem, and requested that the letter be opened and read only if he was murdered on military duty, the duty he felt himself obliged to perform. Like Lord Louis Mountbatten, he paid that supreme sacrifice.

The poem he enclosed with his letter is, I feel, a fitting tribute to all those whose lives were ended in this vile and unforgivable way.

> Forgive me, and forgive those that trespass against me.
> Do not stand at my grave and weep.
> I am not there, I do not sleep.
> I am the thousand winds that blow,
> I am diamond glints on snow.
> I am the sunlight on ripened grain,
> I am gentle autumnal rain.
> When you waken in the morning hush
> I am the soft uplifting rush
> Of quiet birds in circled flight.
> I am the soft stars that shine at night.
> Do not stand at my grave and cry.
> I am not there. I did not die.

Epilogue

'They can write what they like about me when I'm dead.' Whenever he was asked to write his memoirs, and there were many such invitations, that was Lord Louis' reply. Many have written what they liked about him, but without his consent. Much of their writings are untrue and misleading, displaying no knowledge of the great man. None have been in the position I held, so intimately close to him, constantly sharing every moment of every day, in every part of the world, at home, at work and at play.

The great state occasions, the endless tours, the wonderful family life, the personal moments, the fun, the silliness, the sadness – all these we shared. And if there were times, as there were, when I could have cried at the demands being made of me, I knew that, like many others of his staff, I would gladly and easily have given my life for him. He instilled in everyone close to him a feeling of belonging, of being important. It was very much 'in the spirit of the hive'.

I have made no attempt to write a biography, but I hope that this, my memory of the privilege and honour I felt at being a part of history, may help others to understand more fully the personality and compassion, the warmth and the kindness of Lord Louis Mountbatten, surely one of the greatest human beings of our century.

I miss him greatly to this day. Born a prince, in my mind he left us a worthy king.

Appendix One:
Beds I Have Slept In

At Royal Palaces

Belgium	Royal Palace, Brussels (King Baudouin)
Denmark	Fredensborg (King Frederik IX)
Federal Republic of Germany	Wolfsgarten, Frankfurt (Prince Ludwig of Hesse)
Great Britain	Windsor Castle (HM The Queen) (for Garter Ceremony, polo and private weekends)
	Balmoral (for September shoots)
	Sandringham (for winter shoots)
Norway	Skaugum (King Olav V)
Sweden	Drottningholm (King Gustaf VI)
	Ulriksdal
	Sophiero
Thailand (formerly Siam)	Postanuk Guest Palace (King Bhumibol Adulyadej)

At Royal Lodge

Kenya	Sagana

At Governor-General Residences and Government Houses

Aden (now part of Yemen)	
Australia	Canberra, Sydney and Yaramulta
Bahamas	Nassau
Bermuda	
Canada	Ottawa and Victoria, British Columbia

Fiji	Suva
Guyana (formerly British Guiana)	Georgetown
Hong-Kong	
Jamaica	King's House
Jersey (Channel Islands)	
Kenya	Nairobi
Malaysia (North Borneo)	Mount Hagan
Malawi (formerly Nyasaland)	Zomba
New Zealand	
Papua New Guinea	Port Moresby
Sierra-Leone	Freetown
Sri Lanka (formerly Ceylon)	King's Pavilion, Kandy
Tanzania (formerly Tanganyika)	Zanzibar (a separate country when I visited) Dar-es-Salaam
Trinidad	
Zambia (formerly Northern Rhodesia)	Lusaka
Zimbabwe (formerly Southern Rhodesia	Harare (formerly Salisbury), Bulawayo and Broken Hill

At British Embassies and Residencies

Argentina	Buenos Aires
Australia	Canberra
Brazil	Rio de Janeiro
Bahrain	
Brunei	
Chile	Santiago
Cyprus	Episkopi
Federal Republic of Germany	Bad Godesberg
Greece	Athens (for the King's wedding)
New Zealand	Wellington
Nigeria	Kano
Peru	Lima
Singapore	
Turkey	Ankara
United States of America	Washington DC

Venezuela	Caracas
Zambia (formerly Northern Rhodesia)	Ndola

At Presidential Palaces

India	Former Viceroy's House, now Rashtrapati Bhavan, New Delhi
	Raj Bhavan, Bombay
	Viceroy's Summer House, Simla
Liberia	The Executive Mansion, Monrovia
Malaysia	Astana, Kuching, Sarawak
	Istana, Jesselton
	Istana Tetamu, Kuala Lumpur
	Peduase Lodge

Some military bunks

Australia	RAAF Fairburn
Canada	USAF Labrador
	USAF Newfoundland
	St Lawrence Seaway (for Fleet Review on board *HMS Scarborough*)
Cyprus	HQ, Middle East Air Force
France	SHAPE HG, Paris
Great Britain	Royal Naval College, Dartmouth
	Gogar Bank House, Edinburgh
	Royal Yacht *Britannia* (for Cowes Week)
Libya	RAF El Adem
Maldive Islands	RAF Maldive Islands
Philippines	USAF Guam
Singapore	Command House
United States of America	US Navy, San Francisco
	US Navy Honolulu, Hawaii
	Fort Worth (with Texas Rangers)
	Fort Bragg, North Carolina (with US Army Strategic Force)
	Fort Benning (with US Paratroop Corps)
	USAF Offat Air Base, Omaha, Nebraska
	Military Academy, Charlestown, Savannah

I also went round the world (twice!) with the RAF's 216 Squadron

Some top hotels

Bermuda	The Bermudiana (then owned by the Whernhers of Luton Hoo, Lord Mountbatten's cousins)
Brazil	The Naçional, Brasilia
Canada	The Royal York, Toronto (the largest hotel in the Commonwealth)
Kenya	Treetops, Nyeri
Mexico	The Isobella, Mexico City
New Zealand	Otehei Lodge, Bay of Islands
Peru	Cabo Blanco, Talara
USA	The Bright Angel Lodge, Grand Canyon
	The Ahwahnee, Yellowstone
	The Waldorf Astoria (Presidential Suite), New York
Zimbabwe (then Southern Rhodesia)	The Victoria Falls

Appendix Two:
A Selection of Lord Mountbatten's Uniforms (Basic Items Only)

Admiral of the Fleet

Full Ceremonial Blues	Day tails and gold laced trousers; full decorations (maximum 4 stars); 2 neck badges; white gloves
Evening Ball Dress	Evening tails and gold laced trousers; full evening decorations; patent wellingtons
Evening Mess Dress	Evening tails and plain trousers; white waistcoat; miniature medals
Evening Mess Undress	Monkey (short) jacket; black waistcoat and trousers; medal ribbons; patent shoes
Blue Day Uniform	Reefer jacket; medal ribbons; plain-toed black shoes
Semi-Full Dress Blues	Reefer jacket with sword; decorations (maximum 2 stars)
Naval Khaki (Formal)	Khaki tunic, shirt and tie
Naval Khaki (Bush)	Jungle green bush shirt
Full Ceremonial Whites	White linen tunic; full decorations
Tropical Ceremonial Evening Ball Dress	White linen monkey jacket; gold laced trousers white waistcoat; evening decorations; patent shoes
Tropical Mess Dress	Semi-formal white linen monkey jacket; black trousers; white waistcoat; miniature medals
Tropical Mess Undress	White monkey jacket; black waistcoat and trousers; medal ribbons

Red Sea Rig	Short-sleeved white shirt with epaulettes and cummerbund
Tropical Day Dress	White linen tunic; long white trousers; medal ribbons; white buckskin shoes
Tropical Bush Dress	Informal long or short-sleeved white linen tunic; long white trousers or shorts; buckskin shoes

NB Naval boat cloak worn over most of the above.

Colonel The Lifeguards

Full Ceremonial Mounted Review Order	Scarlet tunic; helmet and plumes; white buckskins; thigh boots; white gauntlets; cuirasses (steel breast plates); scarlet cape
Frock Coat	Long black frilled-front frock coat; black overalls (breeches) with broad red stripes; black cap
Khaki Day Dress	Khaki tunic, shirt and tie; Sam Browne belt; cane; khaki cap; brown brogue shoes
Khaki Tropical	Khaki bush jacket, trousers and cap; brown brogues
Full Ceremonial Evening Dress	Scarlet monkey jacket, gold and scarlet waistcoat, black overalls (breeches) with red stripes; patent wellington boots; box stirrups

Colonel Commandant The Royal Marines

Ceremonial Blues	Blue tunic; overalls (breeches with red stripe); white shirt; black tie; Sam Browne belt; white cap
Day dress	Blue tunic; trousers with red stripe; white shirt; black tie; Sam Browne belt; white cap; lanyard
Mess Dress	Red monkey jacket; blue overalls (breeches); black bow tie; decorations; white cap; aiguillettes; patent boots
Khaki Day Dress	Khaki tunic and trousers; khaki shirt and tie; green beret; Sam Browne belt; brown brogues

Elder Brethren Trinity House

| | Naval frock coat; decorations; sword |
| Day dress | Day reefer jacket; medal ribbons |

Royal Thames Yacht Club

Mess dress — Evening monkey jacket and trousers with RTYC buttons; piqué evening shirt; white waistcoat; cap with RTYC badge; black bow tie; patent shoes

Knight of the Most Noble Order of the Garter

Evening breeches — Full evening dress with black breeches, silk stockings and gold garter round knee; stiff dress shirt; wing collar; white bow tie; white dress waistcoat with diamond links and buttons; patent pumps with silk bows; full evening decorations

Appendix Three:
Lord Mountbatten's Robes

The Most Noble Order of the Garter	Mantle of royal blue velvet lined with white satin; maroon cross sash; chapeau (hat) with Prince of Wales plume of ostrich feathers; gold collar (chain) across shoulders. (Worn annually at the Garter Ceremony at Windsor Castle.)
The Imperial Order of the Crown of India	Mantle of turquoise blue with ermine-lined edge and lined with white satin; white silver tassle. (Not worn since Viceregal days.)
The Most Honourable Order of the Bath	Crimson red satin robes. (Only worn for annual ceremony of the Order.)
The Royal Victorian Order	Royal blue robes with maroon striped edging. (Only worn for the annual ceremony of the Order.)
The Coronation Robes	Scarlet robes edged with white ermine; ermine shoulder caps; white silk lining; earl's coronet. (Worn only at the Coronation of the Sovereign.)
The Peer's Parliamentary Robes	Scarlet robes edged with ermine; earl's white ermine bands; black tape bows to tie. (Worn at State Opening of Parliament.)

High Steward of Romsey — Black and dark blue mantle; large chain; star badge; tricorn hat. (Worn on civic duty in the Borough for such events as royal visits.)

NB Lord Mountbatten also wore the mantles of the many universities of which he held honourary doctorates and degrees

Appendix Four:
A Complete List of Lord Mountbatten's Orders and Decorations

Earl Mountbatten of Burma (1947)
Baron Romsey of Romsey (1947)
Knight of the Most Noble Order of the Garter (1946)
The Military Order of Merit (1965)
Knight Grand Cross of the Star of India (with Grand Master's Badge) (1947)
Knight Grand Cross of the Indian Empire (1947)
Knight Grand Cross of the Military Order of the Bath (1955)
Knight Grand Cross of the Royal Victorian Order (1937)
The Distinguished Service Order (1941)
Knight of the Order of St John (1943)

The American Legion of Merit
The American Distinguished Service Medal
The Swedish Order of the Seraphim
The Danish Knight Grand Cross of the Order of Dannebrog
The French Legion of Honour (Grand Cross)
The French Croix de Guerre
The Burmese Order of Agga Maha Thiri Thuddhamma
The Siamese Order of the White Elephant
The Chinese Order Special Grand Cordon of the Cloud and Banner
The Roumanian Order of the Crown and Star
The Greek Military Cross
The Greek Grand Cross of the Order of George I of Greece
The Nepalese Grand Cross of the Order of the Star of Nepal
The Ethiopian Grand Cross of the Order of Solomon
The Portuguese Grand Cross of the Military Order of Aviz
The Netherlands Order of the Lion

Freeman of the City of London (with Sword of Honour) (1946)
Freeman of the City of Edinburgh (1954)
First Freeman of Romsey (1946)

High Steward of Romsey (1940)
Fellow of the Royal Society (1965)
Gold Stick and Colonel The Life Guards (1965)
Colonel Commandant The Royal Marines (1965)
Governor of the Isle of Wight (1965)
Privy Councillor (1947)

Hon. LL D Cambridge University (1946)
Hon. DCL Oxford University (1946)
Hon. DSc Delhi and Patna University (1948)
Hon. Fellow Christ College, Cambridge (1946)
Hon. LL D Leeds University (1950)
Hon. LL D Edinburgh University (1950)
Hon. LL D Southampton University (1955)
Hon. LL D Sussex University (1963)

Index

Abbubarker, 62, 97
Acapulco, 105-6
Aden, 137-8
Alexandra, Princess, 50, 70, 89, 129, 154
Alice, Princess of Greece, 85, 150
Amin, Idi, 145
Andrew, Prince, 47-8, 90
Anne, Princess, 48, 84, 119
Antilles, 161-2
Argentine, 113
Ashley, Wilfrid, 67
Atlantic College, 122
Australia, 101-2

Bahamas, 107-8
Bahrain, 64
Balmoral, 95
Bangkok, 61, 95, 98-100
Baudouin, King of the Belgians, 95
BBC, 24-5
Beatles, 129
Belgium, 95
Bermuda, HMS, 27-8
Bhumibol, King of Thailand, 86
Bingham, Hyram, 110, 111
Birch, Arthur, 84
Blake, George, 127
Bogarde, Dirk, 123
Bokassa, 145
Borneo, 100-1
Brabourne, Lady (Lady Patricia Mountbatten), 89, 100, 117, 133-4, 143, 150
Brabourne, Lord, 117, 123-4, 150-1
Brabourne, Nicholas, 117, 150
Brabourne, Timothy, 117, 150
Brasilia, 112

Brazil, 111-13
Brecknock, Countess of, 77
Brenda, 12-13, 19, 20, 85
Briggs, Johnny, 123
Britannia, HMY, 28-9, 31-2, 37, 43-7
British Legion, 154, 155
Broadlands, 32-3; history, 67; 'Living Museum', 64, 65, 91-2; visitors to, 70-7, 79-81, 83-91, 94
Brockman, Vice Admiral Sir Ronald, 70, 139
Brown, Capability, 67
Brown, George, 139-40
Bryce, Mr and Mrs Ivor, 105, 107
Bulganin, Nikolai, 27
Burma, 63, 64
Bush, Captain, 16, 18

Cadiz, HMS, 16-21, 28
Callas, Maria, 70, 122
Canada, 37-8
Cardinale, Claudia, 86, 124
Caribbean, 45-6, 106-7, 161-2
Cartland, Barbara, 68, 75-6
Cartwright, Captain, 16
Cassel, Maudie, 67
Central African Republic, 145
Ceres, HMS, 16
Chaplin, Charlie, 71-2, 123
Chaplin, Oona, 71
Charles, Prince of Wales, 48, 50, 81, 89-90, 116, 120-1
Chile, 111
Christmas Island, 103-4
Churchill, Sir Winston, 8, 80, 141-3
Cinematographic Society, 123
Classiebawn Castle, 2, 67, 149-57
Colville, Sir John, 141

Commonwealth Immigration Commission, 128, 147
Commonwealth Independence Commission, 147
Constantine, King of the Hellenes, 118–19, 135
Le Corbusier, 112
Coward, Noël, 86, 123
Creasy, Admiral Sir George, 21–3, 26, 28
Crosby, Bing, 124
Cudlipp, Hugh, 126

Dawe, Revd E.L., 6–8
Day, Miss, 49–50
Delhi, 138–9, 141
Denmark, 95
Devine, Andy, 139
Diana, Princess of Wales, 89, 120

Edward, Prince, 90
Elizabeth, Queen Mother, 22, 80, 93, 96, 155
Elizabeth II, Queen, 22, 47–8, 53, 54, 149; reviews Fleet, 23–5; at Broadlands, 73, 75, 79, 84, 89, 93, 116; marriage, 119–20
Ethiopia, 143–4, 145

Fabiola, Queen of the Belgians, 95
Fairbanks, Douglas Jnr, 60–1, 70, 74
Fairbanks, Douglas Snr, 123
Fiji, 103, 147
Fleming, Ian, 107
Ford, Henry II, 74, 77
Frankovitch, Mike, 80, 124–5

Gable, Clark, 124
Gandhi, Mahatma, 141
General Mills Corporation, 145–6
George VI, King, 22, 34, 54, 65
Gloucester, Duke of, 120
Grace, Princess of Monaco, 85, 124
Granger, Stewart, 124
Grant, Cary, 124
Greece, 135
Grotrian family, 10
Guinness, Alec, 123
Gustav, Crown Prince of Sweden, 150
Gustav, King of Sweden, 77–9, 118–19, 133, 152

Haile Selassie, Emperor of Ethiopia, 143, 145
Harrison, Rex, 70
Hawaii, 104–5
Heath, Ron, 162
Heathrow Airport, 128
Hemingway, Ernest, 111
Hepburn, Audrey, 121–2
Hicks, David, 47, 117, 118, 150
Hicks, Edwina, 48
Hicks, Lady (Lady Pamela Mountbatten), 47–8, 117, 150
Hill, Derek, 154
Hirohito, Emperor, 64
Holland, Henry, 67
Hollywood Motion Picture Academy, 80–1
Home, Lord, 139–40
Hong Kong, 100
Honolulu, 104
Hope, Bob, 124

Incas, 110–11
India, 99, 120, 137–41, 144
Indomitable, HMS, 22–3
International Variety Club, 145
Iran, 144–5

Jamaica, 46
James I, King, 73
Japan, 64–5, 142–3, 147
Jenkins, Roy, 127
Jigsaw Club, 154
Juan Carlos, King of Spain, 89

Kauffmann, Angelica, 67
Kelly, HMS, 91–2
Kennedy, John F., 108
Kent, Duke of, 89
Kenya, 52–6
King, Cecil, 125–6
Knapton Hall, 10–12, 20
Khrushchev, Nikita, 27

Laker, Alan 45
Lee Kuan Yew, 98
The Life and Times of Lord Mountbatten, 92, 156
London Weekend Television, 156
Louis, Prince of Hesse, 95
Louise, Queen of Sweden, 63, 77–8, 85, 133–4, 151

Lynn, Vera, 65–6

Maclaine, Shirley, 86, 124
Macmillan, Harold, 70, 156
Maeterlinck, Maurice, 127
Margaret, Princess, 16, 22, 150
Marie, Grand Duchess, 85
Marina, Princess, 160
Mary, Princess Royal, 45, 46
Mary, Queen, 87
MCC, 45
Menzies, Robert, 101
Mexico City, 108–9
Michael, Prince of Gloucester, 89
Ministry of Defence, 58, 128, 156
Mintoff, Dom, 21
Mountbatten, Lord Louis: WE joins personal staff, 32–7; in Canada, 33, 37–8; uniforms, 34–6; in America, 38–41; WE joins staff permanently, 46–7; and his daughter's wedding, 48; nutcases, 49–50; foreign tours, 52–8, 95–114, 133–48; preparations for tours, 58–62; gifts, 62–4; marriage, 68–9; and his wife's death, 69; eating habits, 73–4, 83; dogs, 75; ailments, 76–7; love of cinema, 80–1, 123–5; interest in his family history, 92; Christmas presents, 115–18; London house, 118–19; and Prince Charles, 120–1; Cecil King's plot, 125–7; report on prison security, 127–8; vanity, 127, 129; at Nehru's funeral, 139–41; and Churchill, 141–3; at Classiebawn, 149–57; unification of defence services, 156; WE leaves, 158–62; assassination, 1–2, 164–6
Mohammed Reza Pahlavi, Shah of Iran, 144–5
Montgomery, Field Marshal, 85, 129
Moorea, 133–4
Morley, Peter, 156
Mountbatten, Lady, 33, 91, 96–7, 149; in Canada, 37; treatment of nutcases, 48–9; and Broadlands, 67; marriage, 68–9; death, 46, 47, 51–2, 69, 100
Mullaghmore, 164–6
Mustique, 161–2

NATO, 16–17

Ne Win, General, 64
Nehru, Pandit, 72, 138, 139, 141
Nelson, Lord, 26
Neville, Lord Rupert, 81, 82
New Guinea, 64, 135–7
New Zealand, 102
Nigeria, 62
Norway, 95

Oberon, Merle, 106
Ogilvy, Angus, 70
Olaf, King of Norway, 95
Onassis, Aristotle, 122

Pahlav, Princess, 87
Palmerston, Lord, 67, 149
Pearce, Joe, 139
Pearl Harbor, 104
Peru, 63, 109–11
Philip, Prince, 23–4, 48, 51, 54, 89, 90, 92, 93, 116, 119–20
Pickford, Mary, 123
President, HMS, 91

RAF, 52
Rainier, Prince of Monaco, 85
Reading, Lady, 68
Rio de Janeiro, 112–13
Romsey, 65
Romsey Abbey, 52
Rootes, Lord, 131
Royal Arthur, HMS, 25
Royal Naval College, Osborne, 141–2
Royal Naval Film Corporation, 123

Sagana, 52–3
St Barbe family, 67
St Vincent, HMS, 15–16
Sandhurst, 154–5
Sandringham, 90, 139
Sargent, Sir Malcolm, 86
Scarborough, HMS, 33
Second World War, 3–9, 142
Shadow V, 1–2, 151–2, 154, 164–5
Shastri, Shri Lal Bahadur, 141
Singapore, 64, 98
Sirikit, Queen of Thailand, 86, 99–100
Slim, Field Marshal Lord, 66, 85
Smith, Charles, 48, 75, 83, 90, 117, 160
Sopwith, Lady, 77
Sopwith, Sir Tommy, 77
South America, 107–14

Southern Rhodesia, 52, 57–8
Spiegel, Sam, 80
Strong, Charles, 76
Surprise, HMS, 23–4
Sweden, 78–9, 95

Tahiti, 147
Tassell, Mr, 11, 12, 21
Terraine, John, 156
Thailand, 61, 98–100
Toronto, 37–8
Trasna of Ely, 163
Treetops, 53–6
Trinidad, 45, 106
Trueman, Freddie, 45

Uganda, 52, 144, 145
Ulriksdal, 78
United States, SS, 87
United States of America, 38–40, 145–6

Vanguard, HMS, 22, 23, 24–5, 33
Victoria, Queen, 85
Victory, HMS, 26–7

Walker, Sherbrook, 55
Webb, Commander Ben, 70, 160
Wedgwood, Josiah, 67
Welensky, Sir Roy, 57
West Indies, 45–6, 106–7, 161–2
Westminster, Duke of, 154, 163
Wilson, Bishop, 64
Wilson, Harold, 126, 127
Windsor, Duchess of, 87–9
Windsor, Duke of, 68, 87–9
Windsor Castle, 95–6

Yeats, W.B., 150

Zahra, Chief Petty Officer, 26
Zanzibar, 52
Zuckermann, Solly, 126, 137